AMERICAN BALLET THEATRE

AMERICAN BALLET THEATRE

A 25-YEAR RETROSPECTIVE

Text by Elizabeth Kaye

Foreword by Clive Barnes

A Donna Martin Book

Andrews McMeel Publishing

Kansas City

 For information write
Andrews McMeel Publishing, 4500 Main Street, Kansas City, Missouri 64111.

www.andrewsmcmeel.com

Library of Congress Cataloging-in-Publication Data

Kaye, Elizabeth.
American Ballet Theatre: a twenty-five-year retrospective /
text by Elizabeth Kaye ; foreword by Clive Barnes.
p. cm.

"A Donna Martin book"

ISBN 0-7407-0019-7 (hardcover). — ISBN 0-7407-0018-9 (pbk.)
1. American Ballet Theatre—History. 2. American Ballet Theatre—History
Pictorial works. I. Title.
GV1786.A43K39 1999
792.8'4'0937—dc21 99-21800
CIP

Frontispiece: Othello with Sandra Brown as Desdemona and
Desmond Richardson as Othello (1997). Photo by Roy Round.

American Ballet Theatre: A 25-Year Retrospective
is dedicated to Jacqueline Kennedy Onassis

PHOTO BY MARTHA SWOPE

CONTENTS

The Nutcracker, Act II (McKenzie production) in 1993

ACKNOWLEDGMENTS

American Ballet Theatre: A 25-Year Retrospective
would not have been possible
without the assistance and generosity
of the following:

Richard Braaten Estate
Jack Buxbaum
Anthony Crickmay
Stephen R. Dolan
Kenn Duncan Estate
Nancy Ellison
John Engstead Estate
Richard N. Greenhouse
Gregory Heisler
Paul Kolnik
Bil Leidersdorf
Sue Martin
Pete McArthur
MIRA
Jack Mitchell
Rosalie O'Connor
Louis Peres
David G. Rhoades
Carol Rosegg
Roy Round
Hidemi Seto
Marty Sohl
Martha Swope
Ana Venegas
Jann Whaley

FOREWORD

GREAT BALLET COMPANIES are weird critters. Generally speaking the more they change the more they remain the same, shedding skins like happy, determined reptiles. They are unique among performing arts organizations in that they are completely ongoing and yet, generation after generation of directors, choreographers, ballet masters, teachers, dancers, and indeed, ballets, they absorb, digest, maintain, and develop. The company itself is in a continual and continuous state of flux, forever caught on the cusp of evolution between what it just was and what it is just about to become. Every performance, unique in itself, is some statement of the company's current position, an ever-changing, frequently unreliable balance sheet of its dance and dancers.

The twentieth century, having now dragged itself to a close like a tired old dowager pumping up for the last waltz, was remarkable in dance for witnessing the foundation of three major classic ballet companies—Britain's Royal Ballet and the fraternal yet scarcely identical twins from the United States, American Ballet Theatre and New York City Ballet. Although I was not present at the birth pangs of any of the three, I have been singularly fortunate as a happily paid onlooker (from about 1950 on, I not only got free tickets, but was paid for my pains, or, more likely I think, pleasures) to watch the development of all three—the Royal Ballet from 1942, American Ballet Theatre from 1946, New York City Ballet from 1950. And actually all three have rather more in common than they might care to imagine—and certainly all three have had their ups and downs with, so far at least, the ups always coming out slightly ahead. In the performing arts, particularly in the English-speaking world where there was no royal tradition of their state subvention, survival is always its own reward.

So, to an extent, the story of American Ballet Theatre, and those sixty glorious years, is indeed one of survival. Once Bernard Shaw was asked how he got along with his exuberant movie director Gabriel Pascal. "Not at all badly," Shaw is said to have replied, "but unfortunately, all Pascal really wants to talk about is art, and all I really want to talk about is money." The story of any ballet company is to a large extent about money. Having been vulgar enough, even crass enough, to have mentioned this so early, I shall try to move on, disregard it, and pretend that these sixty years of Ballet Theatre's achievement represent nothing but pure art operating in a perfect world, where audiences automatically attend, bills are automatically paid, and compromises are only in those details that are the work of the devil.

After sixty years of operation it must be obvious that we cannot talk about one ABT—as though it were an organization founded by a thirty-year-old Richard Pleasant, with the formidable assist of Lucia Chase's moderately modest fortune (there, already I've broken my golden rule and mentioned hard cash!), out of the remnants of the Mordkin Ballet in 1939, which gave its first performance on January 11, 1940, and lived happily ever after. Not exactly. Even from the start, there were other backers involved—notably Rudolf Orthwine of *Dance* magazine fame—some associates with the Mordkin Ballet, others with the new venture.

And, of course, after that first season there have in fact been many Ballet Theatres, although one has morphed from the other with the unobtrusive obviousness of shifting cloud formations. Yet—remember what I first said about change and ballet companies—there has always been some, occasionally only residual, sense of Pleasant's original dictum characterized by the initial advertisement for Ballet Theatre, which appeared in December 1939 proclaiming three weeks of performances at the now-destroyed Center Theater. With no undue modesty, and in a phrase dressed up by its first publicity officer, the sometime critic

Amanda McKerrow and Vladimir Malakhov in *La Bayadère*, Act III (1995)

Irving Deakin, it promised: "The Greatest Ballets of All Time Staged by Greatest Collaboration in Ballet History." Ballet Theatre was not going to be a company content to hide its light under a bushel.

I never knew Pleasant, but he must have been a character. He was also no fool. Whether that first company really was the "Greatest Collaboration in Ballet History" is somewhat dubious, although, you know, a strange case could be made for it. Certainly Pleasant, his dreams backed by the ambition and aspiration of Chase, went about his task with unusual perspicacity. Interestingly—and this is one of the oddities of ballet history—when Pleasant first drew up his blueprints for his brave new company, it was not Antony Tudor who was to be invited as a choreographer from London but Frederick Ashton! Pleasant's letter went astray—it was sent to the wrong street and was much later returned "address unknown." Receiving no reply, Pleasant then, on the strong urging of Agnes de Mille, who was already aboard, sent an invitation to Tudor, and the rest is ballet history! Pleasant also tried to negotiate with the likes of George Balanchine and Margot Fonteyn. Fonteyn expressed considerable interest, and since the Second World War, which started in Europe in September 1939, had put a temporary end to the Vic-Wells Ballet (later Sadler's Wells, later the Royal Ballet), thus releasing her from contractual obligations, she indicated that she might well join the new venture. Another possibility approached by Pleasant was a Broadway chorus boy named Gene Kelly, who failed to join Ballet Theatre when he landed a leading role as the Hoofer in William Saroyan's play *The Time of Your Life.* Such are the ploys of chance and the history thus resulting!

The Denver-born, Princeton-educated (he graduated as an architect, incidentally) Pleasant had grandiose plans for his new company, plans which were quite different from the slow-moving Fabian concepts of Lincoln Kirstein and George ("First a School!") Balanchine, who had been laying the careful foundations for New York City Ballet (born, more or less, fully fledged in 1948) ever since Balanchine accepted Kirstein's invitation to come to New York in 1933. Pleasant was a gunslinger, quicker on the draw, less accurate in aim. He instantly recognized the necessity to match in glamour, and therefore in star power, the various Ballets Russes (a corporate term that could at that point cover a variety of sins) then synonymous with large-scale ballet in the United States.

With this in mind he not only hired a few expatriate Russian stars such as Dimitri Romanoff (who as coach and ballet master, and from 1946 as regisseur, was a key figure with ABT until his retirement in 1980), Yurek Shabelevsky, Adolph Bolm, and Anton Dolin—British by birth yet Russian by reputation—but he also engaged among the choreographers Bronislava Nijinska and the father of modern ballet himself, the then-already-ailing Michel Fokine. Later, post-Pleasant, came the addition of the White Russian Irina Baronova and Dolin's partner, another Russo-Brit, the great Alicia Markova.

Pleasant divided the company up into what he termed "Wings"—there was the "Classic" (Dolin and Nijinska), the "Russian" (Bolm, Shabelevsky, Fokine, and a couple of years later, post-Pleasant, Leonide Massine and David Lichine), "American" (Eugene Loring, Agnes de Mille, and later Jerome Robbins and Michael Kidd), "Negro" (which only produced one ballet, de Mille's *Black Ritual*), "Spanish" (Jose Fernandez and, later, Argentinita), and finally "British" (Tudor, Andrée Howard—who like Tudor was a refugee from Britain's Ballet Rambert, but who, unlike Tudor, never succeeded in New York—and, doing double service, the indefatigable Dolin). I would have loved to be a fly on the wall at some of their policy meetings.

The dancers that first season, apart from a few Russians, were not all that famous, but significantly the roster embraced the rising generation of emerging American ballerinas, including Patricia Bowman, Karen Conrad, Viola Essen, and Annabelle Lyon, who, partnered by Dolin, was the company's first Giselle. None of these stayed very long and not one of them was present when I encountered ABT (then just Ballet Theatre) in 1946. However, in the 1939 ensemble —some of them recruited from Broadway, by the way— there were such future luminaries as Miriam Golden, Nora Koreff (who was soon to change her name to Nora Kaye), Leon Danielian, Maria Karnilova, Herbert Bliss, and Donald Saddler. By the summer of 1940 new recruits came in, including Alicia Alonso, Fernando Alonso, Muriel Bentley, Nana Gollner, John Kriza, and Jerome Robbins. And, of course, Tudor had arrived with his principal male dancer, Hugh Laing.

The first season was a smash hit. After the opening, John Martin, writing in the *New York Times*, described it as "the beginning of a new era," while Walter Terry, in the *New York Herald Tribune*, wrote about "the finest performance of Fokine's *Les Sylphides* that New York has seen in many a season." The 3,500-seat Center Theatre was for most of the season completely sold out, and had not the world premiere of the Walt Disney cartoon feature *Pinocchio* been scheduled to open on February 4, this first Ballet Theatre season might have been extended, although the financial practicability of that is disputed by Ballet Theatre's careful chronicler and historian, Charles Payne. Pleasant had originally announced twenty-one ballets for his inaugural season, and actually managed to present eighteen! It was this flying start he had dreamed of, and the solid success he had promised Lucia Chase.

Never meeting Pleasant, who died in 1961 at the age of fifty-six,

I often wondered exactly what he was like. Isadora Bennett (a legendary ballet publicist in her time, who once had Pleasant as a partner in her PR firm) characterized him as "bright, charming, yet abrasive and crafty." Oliver Smith described him to me as "clever, cunning, ambitious but distressingly vague about money." I guess it was vagueness rather than cunning that finally got him. The company's success in New York and later across the country was unquestioned, but the company's sponsors (contrary to popular belief, Chase—although the major backer—was never, after possibly the first season, its sole financial support) just could not provide Pleasant with the money demanded by his aspirations. He commissioned a new Tudor, *Pillar of Fire*, he struggled to involve Doris Humphrey in a new work—which would have been the first collaboration between American classic ballet and American modern dance—and he had other ideas by the dozen. But the money for them was "distressingly vague."

Thwarted, Pleasant left after the second season, his regime officially terminating on March 1, 1941. He should probably have stuck it out—but who knows? With Pleasant gone, the un-Pleasant years started. The great impresario (at this point not so great as he was to become) Sol Hurok needed a ballet company to take on the road, and he made the infant Ballet Theatre an offer it could not refuse. He had it billed as "the greatest in Russian ballet," which must have been a tad discouraging for people already thinking in terms of an American national company—an idea that only finally crystallized in 1946 when the then-management encountered Ninette de Valois's Sadler's Wells Ballet, which subsequently became a partial blueprint. But for the time being it was a Hurok attraction—guest stars were imported and the company was effectively led by Baronova (1941–43), Markova (1941–46), and André Egelvsky (1942–43, briefly returning in 1946), although at the same time, home-developed dancers, particularly Alonso, Kaye, Kriza, the Tudor specialist Laing, plus Robbins, Kidd, and Harold Lang as character dancers, were very much making their presence felt.

During most of the Hurok years Ballet Theatre's director was German Sevastianov, husband of Baronova and an experienced Ballet Russe manager. It was during the Sevastianov/Hurok period that Fokine created his last ballet, *Bluebeard*, with starring roles for Baronova and Dolin. Sevastianov was drafted into the Army in May 1943, and his role as managing director was assumed by the wealthy but blithely amateur J. Alden Talbot, who resigned after difficulties with, among others, Massine, in April 1945. On April 21 of that year Ballet Theatre's Board of Directors appointed Lucia Chase and Oliver Smith, a designer and youthful Broadway producer, administrative directors. But, even before then, the moment had come to split with Hurok. Hurok, in any event, had for the time being decided to say in his own words, "to hell with ballet." The "official" exclusive contract with Hurok actually extended until October 1947, but it was legally set aside in April 1946.

Ballet Theatre, soon to rename itself American Ballet Theatre, was prepared to take over its own destiny. With Chase and Smith at the helm, and with a recruit from the Theatre Guild, Peter Lawrence, installed as executive manager, on June 20 the new Ballet Theatre set sail on the *Queen Mary* to play its first overseas engagement, a nine-week season at London's Royal Opera House, Covent Garden. This was the first foreign visit to be undertaken by an American dance company since Catherine Littlefield's Pennsylvania Ballet went to Europe, including a Covent Garden season in 1937. Ballet Theatre opened, appropriately enough, on July 4, 1946. By this time the posters announced Chase and Smith as directors, and Tudor as artistic administrator. The opening program was *Les Sylphides*, with Eglevsky, Alonso, Kaye, and Barbara Fallis; Robbins's *Fancy Free*, with Kidd, Kriza, and Robbins; Dolin's version of the "Black Swan" pas de deux, with Kaye and Eglevsky; and *Bluebeard*, with Kriza and Chase. Tudor's *Pillar of Fire* had its London premiere the following night, and the season also saw revivals of *Petrouchka* (the first Petrouchka I ever saw was Jerome Robbins, quickly followed by that of Michael Kidd); a number of already familiar Tudor works, plus the London premiere of his *Romeo and Juliet* and *Undertow*; Balanchine's *Apollo*, plus the London premiere of his *Waltz Academy*; Dolin's versions of *Giselle* and *Swan Lake*, Act II; new works such as Agnes de Mille's *Tally Ho* and *Three Virgins and a Devil*; Robbins's *Interplay*; Lichine's *Helen of Troy*; John Taras's *Graziana*; and Michael Kidd's enormously popular *On Stage*. London, as well as my teenage self, was enchanted by the whole season.

This London visit marked the beginning of what was to be basically, with one important amendment, the ABT (it finally took the title American Ballet Theatre in 1957) that would exist until Mikhail Baryshnikov took over the reins in 1980. One important concomitant event of that first London season was the exposure of Chase and Smith to the Sadler's Wells Ballet and its production of *The Sleeping Beauty*. The full-length nineteenth-century classics (*Giselle* apart) had not been properly seen in the United States, and the grandeur of this *Sleeping Beauty*, which, of course, was going to impress American audiences just three years later, when Hurok first brought the Sadler's Wells Ballet to New York, made the ABT management want to match the scope and solidity of this British organization only a few years older than ABT itself. Smith, in particular, became almost obsessed with the idea of a permanent home theater—a concept still not realized—while Chase determined to acquire the full-evening classics.

ABT did not always have a smooth ride. I really only know this from hearsay—and reviews and all that kind of hokum. For a time I saw much more of New York City Ballet and American modern-dance troupes, such as Graham, Limón, Taylor, Cunningham, and Ailey, than I saw of Ballet Theatre. This was only partly chance. In any event I virtually lost touch with the company—except via the public prints, private letters, and desultory gossip—between 1956 and 1965, when I came to live in New York. Things for a time had not gone well for the company, and at times it appeared to be hovering queasily on the brink of extinction, although things started to come around by about the beginning of the '60s. In October 1961, the Danish choreographer Harald Lander staged his *Études* for ABT with a cast led by Toni Lander, Royes Fernandez, and Bruce Marks. This, together with Lander's subsequent production of Bournonville's *La Sylphide* three years later, also with Lander and Fernandez and the first Bournonville ever staged by an American company, suggested a new spirit in the troupe.

The renaissance moved from the realm of hope to fact in 1965 when the company celebrated its Silver Jubilee with a season at Lincoln Center's New York State Theater. The highlight here was the production by Jerome Robbins of Stravinsky's *Les Noces*. Although Robbins had long been semi-associated with ABT in the public mind, he hadn't done anything new for the company for nearly twenty years. *Les Noces* was a mitzvah, and set the seal on the troupe's first quarter-century. ABT was moreover acquiring a much stronger group of principals and soloists, and it was prepared to undertake its next great adventure—the full-evening ballet.

The decision to mount the full-length *Swan Lake* belonged to Chase and Smith alone, who went against the advice of their "advisory artistic board," including both de Mille and Robbins. In 1965 the former Royal Ballet principal, David Blair, had produced a full-evening *Swan Lake* for Robert Barnett's Atlanta Ballet. It was very effective—it was more or less a facsimile of the Nikolai Sergeyev staging of the 1895 Petipa/Ivanov original produced by the Royal Ballet. But the first ABT mounting of the Blair *Swan Lake* was a very bold move, which could easily have had disastrous consequences, and it was a move destined to change forever the basic formula of the ABT repertory. The first performance was given on February 16, 1967, in Chicago with the Royal Ballet's Nadia Nerina as guest artist, partnered by Royes Fernandez.

The scenery was by Smith himself, who deliberately tried in his designs to give the production the air and ambiance of what he termed at the time, an "old-established State ballet troupe." At the end of 1963 he and Chase had been bitterly disappointed when the Ford Foundation grants for dance—the first major grants ever given to dance in this country—were made exclusively to Balanchine, Kirstein, and companies associated with them. Privately—and I suppose quite publicly—both stormed at what they perceived to be the injustice of it. This *Swan Lake* was very much ABT's answer to what they felt had been a marginalization of their efforts, and, interestingly, it was also a move to set them apart from a third company, the markedly smaller but fast-rising Joffrey Ballet, which was then establishing itself as a new but real force on ABT's home (although it was still essentially homeless) turf of New York City.

Another major event of 1967 was the emergence of a new choreographer, potentially the first major discovery since Robbins more than twenty years previous, and himself a Robbins protégé. This was Eliot Feld, who in that first year staged both *Harbinger* and *At Midnight*. Chase and Smith were in seventh heaven. Here was the pattern for the future. *Swan Lake* and Feld. Unfortunately, the plans for Feld came totally adrift. He wanted more power and influence than Chase was prepared to give him, and very soon he was off starting the first of his many companies. At Smith's urgent request he briefly returned for a season and a bit in 1971–72, but it never really worked, and Feld was soon back again, very successfully, doing his own thing.

Yet the company, although still homeless—it twice tried to set up a permanent arrangement with Washington, D.C., the second, and more hopeful, time involving a quite lengthy residency at the then-new Kennedy Center—started to prosper in a way it never had before. Blair produced a striking new *Giselle*, and in New York the company moved around from the New York State Theater to City Center to the Brooklyn Academy of Music. By 1970 it was ready to play its first London season in sixteen years, and had the nerve to open at Covent Garden with that cheekily copycat full-length *Swan Lake*.

Eventually ABT finally settled on the Metropolitan Opera House for its regular long spring season. Naturally there were artistic and financial difficulties—and a major figure, now often forgotten in company annals, was Sherwin Goldman. Nominally president of the Ballet Theatre Foundation during the late '60s and early '70s he was in fact also chief executive and a driving, driven power in the company's direction. Indeed he was such a force that Chase, and to a far lesser extent, Smith, seemed to regard him a threat to their authority. But, like Pleasant before him, Goldman played a major role—it was he, for example, who in 1970 ensured with Chase's compliance that Natalia Makarova, newly defected from the Soviet Union, signed up with Ballet Theatre. I know, because I was in London at the time and he telephoned me to find out her then-secret address and caught the next plane over with a contract.

He also developed the star power of the company generally—as well as introducing Makarova, it was partly under his aegis that Carla Fracci and Erik Bruhn became more and more part of the company. For a time it seemed as though Goldman might be poised to take over ABT completely. Chase and Smith had other ideas on the succession—the favored path seemed to be a joint artistic directorship between Erik Bruhn and David Blair. Not a bad idea, but one which unfortunately disregarded the simple fact that the two men loathed one another. Or perhaps it didn't really disregard that fact—because, looking back, Chase and Smith seemed themselves in no hurry to part company with the company. It was a burden, but it was their burden. And they were extremely good at bearing it.

The company by now was a major international force. True, it lacked a major choreographer, apart from the somewhat attenuated links to Tudor. But it had mounted a range of full-evening ballets, adding *Coppélia,* in a production by Enrique Martinez in 1968, and Rudolf Nureyev's *Raymonda* (in 1975 with a first cast consisting of Cynthia Gregory, Nureyev, and Bruhn), while encouraging a number of young choreographers, notably Michael Smuin and Dennis Nahat. Also in 1970 a first move was made to include modern dance in the repertory with the production of two Jose Limon revivals, *The Moor's Pavane* and *The Traitor,* while Glen Tetley also made significant contributions to the repertory. New dancers were shining, notably Gregory; Martine van Hamel; Marianna Tcherkassky; two recruits from New York City Ballet, Gelsey Kirkland and John Prinz; the male wunderkind, Fernando Bujones, like van Hamel a Gold Medal Winner from the Varna International Dance Competition; more briefly, Michaël Denard from the Paris Opera; and two leading Dutch dancers, Alexandra Radius and Han Ebbelaar.

We are now more or less up to what might be called the Age of Baryshnikov, which is where the present book starts to take up the story. Baryshnikov was twenty-six years old when, on the evening of June 29, 1974, he walked out of the stage door of the O'Keefe Center in Toronto, chose freedom, and slipped into a waiting limousine. The publicity of his choice rang bells around the world, as it had with the previous defectors from Leningrad's Kirov Ballet, Rudolf Nureyev and Natalia Makarova. Soon after, he made his first appearance in the West with the National Ballet of Canada, and a few weeks after that he made his debut with ABT at the New York State Theater. The date was July 27, 1974, the ballet was *Giselle,* the ballerina was Natalia Makarova, the reception was ecstatic.

It is important to remember that the company with which Baryshnikov was throwing in his lot was a very strong troupe. He also appeared with other companies, notably, like Makarova, Britain's Royal Ballet, but ABT became his home base. That same year, Tudor—always called by Oliver Smith "the conscience of American Ballet Theatre"—had, after a long absence spent both teaching at Juilliard and with various spells with the Royal Swedish Ballet, officially returned with the title of associate director. It was also in 1974 that Natalia Makarova first mounted on ABT "The Kingdom of the Shades" scene from *La Bayadère.* A year later Tudor staged his first ballet for the company in a quarter of a century, *The Leaves Are Fading* for Gelsey Kirkland and Jonas Kage, which is generally regarded as a masterpiece.

The roster of principals, even apart from Baryshnikov himself, was mightily impressive: Karena Brock, Erik Bruhn, Fernando Bujones, William Carter, Eleanor D'Antuono, Carla Fracci, Cynthia Gregory, Gelsey Kirkland, Ted Kivitt, Natalia Makarova, Ivan Nagy, Dennis Nahat, Terry Orr, Marcos Paredes, John Prinz, Marianna Tcherkassky, Clark Tippet, Martine van Hamel, Charles Ward, Sallie Wilson, and Gayle Young. For the company's thirty-fifth anniversary gala in January and July 1975 the company not only showed off all of these dancers, but also variously Alicia Alonso, partnered by Jorge Esquivel in *Swan Lake,* Act II, pas de deux; Rudolf Nureyev partnering Kirkland in the *Corsaire* pas de deux; Bruhn, Gregory, and Nureyev in Bournonville's *La Ventana* pas de trois; and Gregory in *The Sleeping Beauty* "Rose Adagio" partnered by a quartet including Andre Eglevsky and Igor Youskevitch. Other guest artists around that time included Noella Pontois, Lynn Seymour, and Paolo Bortoluzzi. Unquestionably Baryshnikov added luster to even a star assemblage such as this, but he did not shine in solitary splendor.

The Baryshnikov period with ABT was not unbroken. In 1978 he left ABT to dance with New York City Ballet—his first appearance with his new company being in July at Saratoga—then the following November he made his New York debut with the Balanchine troupe. Then suddenly in 1980, with Balanchine's blessing, he left, invited by the ABT board to become the new artistic director of American Ballet Theatre. It was a surprise—indeed such a surprise that Baryshnikov took the unusual measure of announcing it personally to certain members of the press.

The nine years of Baryshnikov's directorship proved fruitful and controversial. Baryshnikov introduced many new dancers into the company, such as Alessandra Ferri and Guillaume Graffin, and he also encouraged such less experienced talent as Susan Jaffe, the tragically doomed Patrick Bissell, Kevin McKenzie, Cynthia Harvey, Amanda McKerrow, Leslie Browne, Robert La Fosse, Robert Hill, Danilo Radojevic, Johan Renvall, and Cheryl Yeager. Soon after he joined ABT, Baryshnikov prevailed upon Chase and Smith to commission Twyla Tharp to create *Push Comes to Shove,* which was premiered at the beginning of 1976. As director Baryshnikov brought Tharp closer into the ABT fold, appointing her artistic associate, along with the British choreographer Sir Kenneth MacMillan, who staged his Royal Ballet productions of *Romeo and Juliet* and *Manon* as well as a new production of *The*

Sleeping Beauty. He also introduced revivals by Merce Cunningham and Paul Taylor. Of less interest, or lasting value, were his flirtations with post-modern choreographers such as David Gordon and Karole Armitage, although he secured a major success in asking Mark Morris to create *Drink to Me Only with Thine Eyes.*

It is too early to assess fully the Baryshnikov years. Undeniable however, is the fact that he did much to focus public attention on the company and give it a possibly needed shot of celebrity glamour.

Through it all, American Ballet Theatre has survived—and the following pages pay tribute to the glories of its happy present and its glorious immediate past. The company, currently under the direction of Kevin McKenzie, is in good shape and in good hands. But you should be warned that in our present world any ballet company is a giddy thing, a tiny ship easily disturbed by the winds of fashion, even capsized by the tempests of finance. It's come a long way in sixty years—now for the next forty to the centennial. It should be home safe, but as I told you at the outset, ballet companies are weird critters. And there will always be treacherous currents in the ocean. So, good luck!

Clive Barnes

AMERICAN BALLET THEATRE

PHOTO BY MARTHA SWOPE

Mikhail Baryshnikov in *Push Comes to Shove* (1976)

PHOTO BY MARTHA SWOPE

Swan Lake with Cynthia Gregory and Rudolf Nureyev (1978)

PHOTO BY MARTHA SWOPE

Cynthia Gregory and Erik Bruhn in *The Moor's Pavane* (1977)

PHOTO BY MARTHA SWOPE

Gelsey Kirkland and Mikhail Baryshnikov in *Giselle,* Act II (1977)

PHOTO BY MARTHA SWOPE

Martine van Hamel as Myrta and Mikhail Baryshnikov as Albrecht in *Giselle,* Act II (1977)

Cynthia Gregory at her Twentieth Anniversary Gala (1985)

PHOTO BY MIRA

PHOTO BY KENN DUNCAN

Johan Renvall as the Bronze Idol in *La Bayadère* (1980)

Natalia Makarova and Anthony Dowell in the "bedroom" pas de deux from *Manon* (1979)

PHOTO BY MARTHA SWOPE

PHOTO BY MARTHA SWOPE

La Bayadère, Act I, Scene I (1980)

PHOTO BY MARTHA SWOPE

Gelsey Kirkland and Mikhail Baryshnikov in Baryshnikov's *The Nutcracker*, taped for broadcast in Toronto (1977)

PHOTO BY MARTHA SWOPE

Raymonda (1980)

PHOTO BY MARTHA SWOPE

Firebird (1977)

PHOTO BY MARTHA SWOPE

La Bayadère, Act II (1980)

PHOTO BY GREGORY HEISLER

Cynthia Harvey as Gamzatti in *La Bayadère* (1980)

PHOTO BY KENN DUNCAN

Fernando Bujones in *La Sylphide* (1983)

PHOTO BY MARTHA SWOPE

Baryshnikov production of *Cinderella* with (left to right) Robert La Fosse, Magali Messac, and Victor Barbee (1983)

PHOTO BY MARTHA SWOPE

Leslie Browne and Robert La Fosse in *Romeo and Juliet,* Act I (1985)

Leslie Browne as Gamzatti in *La Bayadère*, Act I, Scene III (1986)

Romeo and Juliet (1985)

Chapter One

BALLET THEATRE—FROM THE BEGINNING

A BALLET COMPANY is a confluence of individuals whose particular gifts endow it with a spirit and, ultimately, an identity. The process by which it comes of age is gradual and extended. A company matures as a person does: it develops in fits and starts, through determinations and inclinations that lead forward as well as backward, causing it to turn dull at certain junctures and, at others, to experience a restoration. The brevity of each dancer's career assures that a new generation will arise every ten years or so; with each generation, a fresh identity is forged. In that sense, to trace the history of American Ballet Theatre over any given period of time is to trace a succession of companies, each of which profoundly affects the next while possessing its own distinguishing features.

Established in 1939, American Ballet Theatre enjoyed a renaissance in the final years of the twentieth century, just prior to the company's sixtieth year of existence. It was at this point that it fully accomplished its founder's intent: to offer preeminent works performed by unparalleled dancers.

If there was a particular moment that evidenced this achievement, it came on a chilly autumn afternoon in 1997, when the company gathered to film excerpts from the current repertory for the Public Broadcasting System series *Dance in America.* As that day progressed, even an untrained eye could discern that Ballet Theatre had attained a level of artistry that distinguished it from all other companies. For while many of its ballets were staples in opera houses from St. Petersburg to Melbourne, these works seemed crisper, brighter, and deeper when Ballet Theatre danced them. To anyone observing the company that day, the reason for this must have been apparent—Ballet Theatre had become what a great company must be: a venue where technique is so pure, clean, and ingrained that dancers are free to direct their energies toward the artist's primary goal of effecting magic.

PHOTO BY MARTHA SWOPE

Swan Lake (1996)

PHOTO BY MARTHA SWOPE

Mikhail Baryshnikov's 1988 production of *Swan Lake*

PHOTO BY MARTY SOHL

Giselle, Act II (1987)

PHOTO BY DAVID G. RHOADES

Kevin McKenzie as Candy Cane in Mary Day's production of *The Nutcracker* for Washington School of Ballet (1970)

Thus, ABT's audiences enter a mystical domain where reality can be set aside as errant lovers are beckoned to dance themselves to death, as the god Apollo heeds his father's call, as demonically driven creatures enact a rite of spring, as Indian warriors are enchanted by exquisite visions and princes are besotted by delicate white swans. This was ballet as fable, enrichment, and cautionary tale. It proved what this fugitive art form can accomplish when infused with power, nuance, and meaning.

BALLET IS A PARADOX. Eloquent yet wordless, immediate yet timeless, impelling yet surpassingly graceful, it traffics in equal measures of bodily prowess and spiritual transcendence. Danseurs appear to float through the air, seemingly as strong as they are weightless; ballerinas pirouette and poise in arabesque, exemplars of delicacy and endurance. The dancers' skills, wedded to the mastery of choreographers, invest ballet with its uncommon potential to enchant, to provoke, to touch a chord. Yet these ideals are achieved by only the scant number of ballet companies that can qualify as extraordinary.

The art of ballet is passed along in that most intimate of ways: from one individual to another. This means that the past abides as both example and inspiration and that the dancers of "then" are indivisible from the dancers of "now." To apprehend the influences brought to bear on the ABT of the millennium, it is necessary to

Carla Fracci and Erik Bruhn in *Giselle*

glance back more than three decades earlier, when Ballet Theatre's roster included two sublime artists, Carla Fracci and Erik Bruhn, who led the cast of *Giselle* during the company's annual engagement in Washington, D.C. Their performances were attended by a small and eager ballet student with inquiring hazel eyes who would become enamored with ballet while observing these exceptional dancers. His name was Kevin McKenzie. Eight years later, having acquired the skills, look, and manner of a *danseur noble*, McKenzie joined ABT as a principal dancer. Two years after that, when the company again performed in Washington, D.C., he was selected to dance Prince Siegfried in a revival of *Swan Lake*. Twelve years later, having retired from ABT, McKenzie returned to assume artistic directorship of the company, on whom he planned to mount his own production of *Swan Lake* in the year 2000. And this magical and eloquent production would reflect convictions about what ballet must be that took root at those long-ago performances that left him spellbound.

As it happens, McKenzie's own dancing career occurred under the artistic direction of Mikhail Baryshnikov, whose tenure in that post lasted from 1980 to 1989. During those years, Baryshnikov's desire to expand and enhance the technical and artistic scope of the company's repertory and dancers was matched by his readiness to thwart any convention that deterred him from those ends. Baryshnikov knew that, as a rule, young dancers are not taken into major companies as principal dancers, but he dispensed with that custom when he saw youthful dancers with remarkable qualities. One was Alessandra Ferri, a preternaturally gifted dramatic ballerina whose performances offered passage into the vagaries of the human heart. Another exception was made for Guillaume Graffin, an elegant and romantic embodiment of that defining figure, the ballet prince.

In 1986, Baryshnikov also bestowed principal rank on a nineteen-year-old Argentine who had recently won the gold medal at the Fifth International Ballet Competition in Moscow. His name was Julio Bocca. As years passed, he would substantiate Baryshnikov's early faith in him by developing into an artist regarded by many as the world's leading virtuoso. A year after Bocca joined the company Baryshnikov was preparing a production of his much-lauded version of *Don Quixote* and coached Bocca in the leading role of Basilio. A demanding part that called for the utmost in panache and effervescence, it is a role that can seal a young danseur's reputation, or diminish it.

Baryshnikov's own success in the role was such that when he performed it, both prior to his defection and after it, he invariably created a sensation. When the time came for him to teach it to Julio Bocca, his ability to convey what molded his performance was

PHOTO BY CAROL ROSEGG

Paloma Herrera and Julio Bocca dance the 1995 world premiere of Kevin McKenzie and Susan Jones's staging of *Don Quixote*

instrumental in making Basilio one of the roles for which Bocca would be most renowned.

Eight years later, Bocca would again be coached for the role of Basilio, this time for a new ABT production choreographed by Kevin McKenzie and Susan Jones. At the premiere, he partnered another young Argentine dancer, Paloma Herrera, who was twenty at the time. Growing up in Buenos Aires, Miss Herrera had been transfixed by videotapes of American Ballet Theatre that featured Baryshnikov, Natalia Makarova, Martine van Hamel, Cynthia Gregory, and McKenzie. The uncommon caliber of these artists fueled her determination to dance with ABT. And so it proceeds, an ongoing chain of inspiration, yearning, and resoluteness that permits a company to expand, to prevail, to evolve.

PHOTO BY MARTHA SWOPE

Elizabeth Ashton with Lucia Chase and Nora Kaye in *Pillar of Fire* at the Thirty-fifth Anniversary Gala (1975)

By 1975, the occasion of its thirty-fifth anniversary, the company was still enclosed within the embracing and sheltering wing of its patroness and longtime codirector, the formidable Lucia Chase. In her years as a Ballet Theatre dancer, Miss Chase had not been especially accomplished, though she had a gift for mime roles in both comedy and drama. And she brimmed with a love of dance and with that peculiarly American trait known as "pluck," which gave her a sense of possibility and daring along with the driving energy to use those qualities to create something concrete. In the late 1930s she wisely allied herself with Richard Pleasant, a ballet lover with intellect and exceptional taste who had the concept that led to the founding of Ballet Theatre. Pleasant envisioned a company that would serve as an international gallery for all aspects of dance theater. Ballet Theatre soon became an artistic haven where the present fused with the past, where traditional works were illuminated and enhanced with fresh attributes, and where classicism provided a basis on which to found new modes of expression. As such, Ballet Theatre presented nineteenth-century classics, and commissioned new works garnered from the twentieth century's most gifted choreographers, among them George Balanchine, who created the perfectly shaped *Theme and Variations* on the company in 1947, and Jerome Robbins, whose first work, *Fancy Free*, was created for ABT in 1944.

Most particularly, there were ballets from Antony Tudor, who found the ideal exponents for his starkly psychological works in Hugh Laing, a danseur with a singular stage presence, and in Nora Kaye, a pupil of the legendary Michel Fokine, whose choreography for the Ballet Russe signaled the direction ballet would take in the twentieth century. Miss Kaye was a soloist with Ballet Theatre in 1942 when Tudor cast her as Hagar in his *Pillar of Fire*, a new work in which other roles were danced by Laing, Tudor, and Miss Chase. Miss Kaye's performance was an unlikely combination of subtlety and seething, volcanic tension. It heralded the nascence of a dancer who would become one of the century's leading dramatic ballerinas.

PHOTO BY LOUIS PERES

Antony Tudor

PHOTO BY MIRA

Agnes de Mille coaching Amanda McKerrow for *The Other* (1992)

The early Ballet Theatre also presented many works by Agnes de Mille, who began her lengthy career as a dancer but made her name as the choreographer of lasting works of ballet and of Broadway musicals, among them *Carousel, Brigadoon,* and *Oklahoma!* Between 1940 and 1988, the company danced fourteen of her ballets, the most notable of which were *Three Virgins and a Devil, The Informer,* the exuberant *Rodeo,* and *Fall River Legend,* a recounting of the agonized life of the murderous Lizzie Borden. Of these, *Fall River Legend,* created in 1948, and *Rodeo,* staged for ABT in 1950, had special significance for a company that would eventually declare itself to be "American." Like *Fancy Free* and *Pillar of Fire,* they eschewed ballet's familiar world of make-believe and drew instead upon recognizable contemporary characters who embodied the spirit, tensions, and particular preoccupations of a young country shaping its identity in the ever-shifting kaleidoscope that was the postwar world. In the process, they imbued a traditional art form with that vivid contemporary edge that would prove characteristic of so many of Ballet Theatre's acquisitions.

The Thirty-fifth Anniversary Gala celebrated this rich tradition with an impressive display of classic and contemporary styles.

PHOTO BY MARTHA SWOPE

Fancy Free at the Thirty-fifth Anniversary Gala, with Fernando Bujones, Terry Orr, Buddy Balough, and Jerome Robbins, John Kriza, and Harold Lang (1975)

Cynthia Gregory's "Rose Adagio" was a study in the way that charm enhances classical perfection. Lucia Chase and Nora Kaye re-created their roles in Tudor's *Pillar of Fire*. *Fancy Free*'s three sailors were danced by Buddy Balough, Terry Orr, and Fernando Bujones, who were joined onstage for the curtain call by the ballet's brilliant original cast of Harold Lang, John Kriza, and Robbins, originators of the sailors and models for them. But thirty-one years had passed since *Fancy Free* premiered on ABT's stage. Now, they were middle-aged gentlemen in tuxedos graciously bowing to three considerably younger men clad in costumes they once wore. This was ballet continuity made visible, a demonstration that dancers change but works endure, and that each dancer brings to a work new strengths and weaknesses, shifts in tone, emphasis, and nuance.

A TELLING MEASURE of the regard in which Ballet Theatre was held in the 1960s and '70s is that the most celebrated dancers of that time, those who had defected from the Soviet Union, all found their way to ABT. Tantalized by the repertory's extraordinary

PHOTO BY MARTHA SWOPE

Cynthia Gregory and Rudolf Nureyev dance the leading roles in the American Ballet Theatre premiere of Nureyev's *Raymonda* in 1975

breadth, Nureyev, Baryshnikov, and Natalia Makarova, all gifted and intellectually curious artists, saw the company as opportunity made manifest.

Nureyev performed as a guest artist with Ballet Theatre over the years. The ultimate ballet prince, who danced with scorching abandon, he was his art's most carnal practitioner and its most spiritual. As Nijinsky was before him, he was not merely a dancer but a living embodiment of The Dance. Termed a perfectionist, he took issue with that description, insisting that his goal was strictly the attainment of his ideal. "Perfection is sterile," he said. "My ideal is not somebody else's perfection."

He returned to ABT in 1975 to stage *Raymonda,* the full-length ballet originally choreographed by Marius Petipa in 1898, which Nureyev had previously mounted on the Royal Ballet. A tale of the persistence of heroism and love in the presence of evil, his *Raymonda* was lavish, lyrical, and brash. As Nureyev's first staging of a full-length Petipa work, it showcased and paid homage to the facets of ballet that he held dearest: Petipa, classicism, and himself.

Nureyev took the role of the hero Jean de Briènne, while casting Erik Bruhn as the evil Saracen Abdul-Rakhman, and casting two extraordinary Ballet Theatre ballerinas, Cynthia Gregory and Martine van Hamel, as, respectively, Raymonda and Clemence.

PHOTO BY MARTHA SWOPE

Gelsey Kirkland and Rudolf Nureyev in the pas de deux from *Le Corsaire* (1975)

PHOTO BY LOUIS PERES

Natalia Makarova and Ivan Nagy in *Giselle* (1973)

Later, in the same ballet, Nureyev partnered Gelsey Kirkland, with whom he also danced the pas de deux from *Le Corsaire* at an ABT gala performance in 1975. By then, Miss Kirkland was twenty-two and in the full bloom of her youth and powers, while Nureyev was no longer the shockingly beautiful boy that Dame Margot Fonteyn once described as "a young lion leaping." Approaching forty, he hoped to find in Miss Kirkland that intoxication of youth and genius that Fonteyn had discovered in him fifteen years before. This was not to be. Still, Miss Kirkland would later write that he had "transformed steps into fire." And their dancing was steeped in the entrancement that allows certain fleeting ballet performances to sear themselves into memory.

MISS MAKAROVA made her debut with Ballet Theatre in 1970, dancing Giselle, a role she managed to infuse with the breathtaking ethereality of Dame Alicia Markova and the earthy, Soviet realism that had distinguished the performance of Galina Ulanova.

PHOTO BY MARTHA SWOPE

Natalia Makarova and Ivan Nagy in the 1977 production of *Firebird*

PHOTO BY MIRA

Natalia Makarova and Anthony Dowell in *Swan Lake* (1979)

PHOTO BY MARTHA SWOPE

Anthony Dowell in *Giselle* (1978)

Albrecht was danced by Ivan Nagy, an elegant, Hungarian-born *premier danseur* with a manner at once courtly and regal, strong and tender.

Makarova was an exacting artist who brought verismo to whatever she danced, even fanciful roles like the title role in Fokine's *The Firebird*, for which Ivan Nagy was again her partner. Her Odette/Odile in *Swan Lake* was a revelation. No white swan could be more tender; no black swan could be more enticingly venal. These portrayals illuminated the respective meanings of "bruised" and "bruising," and were danced with a ferocity, facility, and grace that reinforced a general sense in the ballet community that the Kirov's superlative training produced a rare breed of dancer. A different training was to be had at Britain's Royal Ballet, though it too gave rise to extraordinary dancers, one of the most heralded of which was Anthony Dowell.

Dowell, protégé of the Royal Ballet's brilliant choreographer and artistic director Sir Frederick Ashton, came to dance with ABT in 1977. He stayed for three years, then returned to London, where he eventually succeeded Ashton as the Royal Ballet's artistic director. Partnering Miss Makarova in *Swan Lake* and *Giselle*, his performances were an eloquent, unexpected blend of force and vulnerability.

Dowell's most memorable role may have been Solor in *La Bayadère*, which capitalized on his dramatic flair and on his wingedness. This lush, four-act ballet, which Petipa created in 1877, was set on ABT by Miss Makarova in 1980. Previously, she had mounted *La Bayadère*'s mesmerizing "Shades" scene on ABT's corps de ballet, but this was a far more ambitious resurrection of an intricate and magnificent work long performed by the Kirov, but previously unseen in the West. Employing stunning pas de deux, magnificent solos, and lyrical work by the corps de ballet, *La Bayadère*, a saga of the collision between duty and desire, is rife with desperately feuding characters, fatal intrigue, deadly snakes, and a glimpse of perfection in the hereafter.

Makarova danced Nikiya, the sinuous temple dancer overcome by love for the warrior Solor. The Rajah's beautiful, conniving daughter, Gamzatti, was danced by Cynthia Harvey, a promising soloist who went on to be a principal dancer, while the Rajah was portrayed by Victor Barbee, one of the most brilliant dance actors to appear with Ballet Theatre. Alexander Minz played the intractable High Brahmin, while Johan Renvall took the fleeting but dazzling role of the Bronze Idol. This supreme production became a staple of ABT's repertory. Its unrelenting technical and artistic demands have never ceased to challenge the company's artists. And it has given Miss Makarova something that a dancer's career provides but rarely: an enduring place, an enduring presence.

PHOTO BY MARTHA SWOPE

Natalia Makarova's *La Bayadère* (1980) with Cynthia Harvey, Anthony Dowell, and Miss Makarova

PHOTO BY MARTHA SWOPE

The final dress rehearsal for the 1988 production of *Gaîté Parisienne.* Pictured, center, left to right: Costume designer Christian Lacroix, Lorca Massine, artistic director Mikhail Baryshnikov, Susan Jaffe as the Glove Seller

PHOTO BY MARTHA SWOPE

Susan Jaffe in *Symphonie Concertante* (1983)

PHOTO BY MARTHA SWOPE

The Mollino Room, with scenery and costumes by David Salle (1986)

PHOTO BY MIRA

Cheryl Yeager and Julio Bocca in *Don Quixote (Kitri's Wedding)*, Act I (1987)

PHOTO BY MIRA

Cheryl Yeager in *Theme and Variations* (1989)

PHOTO BY MARTHA SWOPE

Ross Stretton and Martine van Hamel (center) in *Raymonda* (1988)

PHOTO BY MARTHA SWOPE

Cynthia Harvey and Kevin McKenzie in *Theme and Variations* (1986)

After his defection, Mikhail Baryshnikov gave his first ABT performance on July 27, 1974, appearing with Natalia Makarova in *Giselle*

PHOTO BY BIL LEIDERSDORF

Leslie Browne and Mikhail Baryshnikov in *The Turning Point* (1977)

PHOTO BY MARTHA SWOPE

Chapter Two

THE BARYSHNIKOV YEARS

It may be that no dancer has had a more profound effect on American Ballet Theatre than Mikhail Baryshnikov, whose meticulous artistic standards and attention to minute detail made him an exemplar for the dancers who worked with him, and for those who came after. Baryshnikov was twenty-six years old when he made his 1974 debut with the company, dancing Albrecht to Makarova's Giselle in a performance that endures as one of the memorable nights that ballet occasionally offers, when dancers exceed the audience's most exalted expectations and the strictures of human possibility.

Still, it did not seem likely, on that warm summer night, that this youthful and most recent Soviet defector would become Ballet Theatre's artistic director in six years. All that was certain was that Baryshnikov brought to ballet something more than the sum of steps brilliantly executed. Like Nureyev, Baryshnikov was an incarnation of ballet's intangibles, that fervency and rapture conveyed through movement, yet born in the spirit and the heart.

The scope and significance of Baryshnikov's achievements were destined to be more apparent to others than to himself. Dance did not come effortlessly to him, but it came easily enough to fuel his view that classical dance was a craft, not an art. As such, the respect he held for it was conditional. Though he was obsessed with ballet and devoted to it, deriving from it fantastic joys and frustrations, he also seemed vaguely embarrassed by it, like a man who cannot stop loving a woman he perceives as disreputable. And his unprecedented fluidity and inborn facility kept him from regarding his work for what it was. "Classical dance was in my pocket," he said, dismissively.

Others assessed him more accurately. "If he couldn't do a movement," Twyla Tharp said of him, "it meant it couldn't be done by anybody, anywhere in the world." But it seemed that there was nothing that he could not do. His gifts were capable of assaying every conceivable style. He always insisted that he owed much to timing, that the virtuoso's path had been paved for him by Erik Bruhn, Edward Villella, Nureyev, and Peter Martins. "I was lucky," he insisted. That was true, though luck was the least of it.

Of ballet dancing he sometimes said, "It's a cool profession." And he was a surpassingly cool dancer who could perform, as the dance critic Arlene Croce noted, with "Olympian detachment." That distance might have separated him from his audience; instead, it made him an object of perpetual yearning. And it lent him the elusive quality that a great star augments with the ability to reveal himself at will. Still, by choice and by temperament, he remained essentially enshrouded. This tantalized audiences unaccustomed to seeing elusiveness on a ballet stage where the custom was to express oneself in broad strokes.

Baryshnikov was more akin to the most interesting postwar film stars Montgomery Clift and James Dean, moody men who turned the term "sensitive man" into something other than an oxymoron. This kinship lent a certain inevitability to Baryshnikov's foray into film, an enterprise previously attempted by only a handful of dancers, who, with the exception of *The Red Shoes*' Moira Shearer, met with limited success. Nureyev's screen portrayals, for example, lacked the dazzling imperiousness he commanded onstage, and his spoken dialogue tended to reinforce the unique power of silence.

But Baryshnikov's ballet persona fitted the screen, especially because he played parts that resembled himself in three of the four films he made, for which he was cast as a melancholic ballet star from the Soviet Union. These films were *White Nights*, *Dancers*, and most notably, *The Turning Point*, a film that popularized both ballet and Baryshnikov as they had never been before. As it happens, the director of *The Turning Point* and *Dancers* was Herbert Ross, who previously had choreographed for Ballet Theatre, and

PHOTO BY MARTHA SWOPE

Mikhail Baryshnikov in Twyla Tharp's *Push Comes to Shove* (1976)

whose executive producer was his wife, Nora Kaye, the former ABT ballerina.

Ross was the first to capitalize on the onscreen potential that made Baryshnikov the first danseur to become a film star. Though he later disparaged his film career ("What career?" he would ask), he was, in fact, that rare, much-touted phenomenon: he was a natural. By turns, puppylike, bright-eyed, or frankly sensual, he could be a troubled and brooding presence, his cornflower-blue eyes veiled in a sorrow that could not be mitigated, as if he sensed that all that has gone wrong can never be set right.

As noted by Joan Acocella, the dance writer who has written about Baryshnikov most perceptively, his essential aspect was that of a loner. There is no reason to surmise that he wanted it otherwise, or that he had a choice in the matter, for his abundant gifts set him apart. As he grew older, he applied himself to modern dance and gave solo performances. They suited him. In the end, he was an artist who had never wholly belonged to anything.

As Acocella has pointed out, it was these qualities that Twyla Tharp drew on when she began creating ballets for him in 1976. The first, *Push Comes to Shove*, established Tharp and Baryshnikov as the right partnership at the right moment. Tharp recently had worked with the Joffrey Ballet and was turning away from modern dance while Baryshnikov was anxious to extend the boundaries of classicism by attempting contemporary dance forms. In those senses, they had started out from opposite places to arrive at a similar spot.

Baryshnikov's initial reaction to Tharp's work was recalled in *Baryshnikov at Work*, a book edited by Baryshnikov's ABT associate, Charles France. As France recalled it, he was immediately compelled by what he saw, by the seriousness he perceived in it, and most especially by what he described as Tharp's "personal understanding of music."

Working with Tharp was a daring venture, even for Baryshnikov, who had never been afraid to attempt something new because he

PHOTO BY MARTHA SWOPE

Roland Petit's *Carmen*, staged for ABT in 1981, with Natalia Makarova and Mikhail Baryshnikov

PHOTO BY MARTHA SWOPE

Gelsey Kirkland and Mikhail Baryshnikov in *La Fille Mal Gardée* (1974)

was aware that he was apt to succeed at any dance form he tried. "In classical ballet I more or less know what the possible is," he said at the time, "but in this case I had no idea what I could or couldn't do."

That, potentially, was the danger in taking on *Push Comes to Shove.* It also explains the sheer joy he derived from it. "A lot of the work I first did in the West was new to me," he would say in *Baryshnikov at Work,* "but nothing was as new, as different . . . as *Push Comes to Shove.*"

BARYSHNIKOV'S body of work embraced the greater part of the canon available to a virtuoso danseur. There was his intense ardor in Roland Petit's highly stylized *Carmen.* There was his madly exuberant hero in the world's oldest ballet, *La Fille Mal Gardée,* a light ballet in the classical vaudeville tradition that allowed him to dance in a style that he had never attempted previously. There was his bedazzled poet in Balanchine's *La Sonnambula,* a work of stunning mystique, delicacy, and power.

In 1976, Jerome Robbins made a pas de deux for Baryshnikov

PHOTO BY SUE MARTIN

La Sonnambula with Chrisa Keramidas and Mikhail Baryshnikov (1981)

PHOTO BY MARTHA SWOPE

Le Spectre de la Rose with Marianna Tcherkassky and Mikhail Baryshnikov (1977)

PHOTO BY MARTHA SWOPE

Mikhail Baryshnikov in *Petrouchka* (1977)

and Makarova. *Other Dances,* later taken into ABT's repertory, was a delectable, extended flirtation danced to a waltz and four mazurkas by Chopin. Following the structure of a grand pas de deux, it was not without eccentricities, as when Robbins included the moment in rehearsal when Baryshnikov lost his spot while turning, became disoriented, and then resumed turning. Robbins was a surpassing perfectionist with an infallible sense of the interworkings between music and steps. For Baryshnikov, working with him was a revelation. "Basically the whole ballet is just a musical idea," Baryshnikov said at the time. "Jerry understands it that way."

Two of Baryshnikov's most resonant renderings were characters Michel Fokine created on Nijinsky. One was the unearthly creature in *Le Spectre de la Rose,* an incorporation of flesh and spirit, a being both romantic and erotic. The other Nijinsky role was *Petrouchka,* a puppet perceived by Fokine as a captive soul

PHOTO BY MARTHA SWOPE

Mikhail Baryshnikov in *Vestris* (1975)

seeking to slough off his chains and, as such, a metaphor for the refusal of living souls to succumb to attempts to defeat them.

Vestris, a work Baryshnikov commissioned for himself in 1969, when he was entering the International Moscow Competition, was another ballet that capitalized on his technical and emotional latitude. Even then, Baryshnikov was fixed on testing the boundaries of his talent. With that in mind, the choreographer he chose was Leonid Jacobsen, once a dancer with the Kirov, who used a variety of complex movement styles while devising steps and characterizations that could call forth new facets of a performer.

The ballet's subject, August Vestris, a danseur at the close of the eighteenth century, had been the first virtuoso. Later he was ballet's most influential teacher and as such the individual from whom all other danseurs descended. Jacobsen's ballet was a tour de force replete with virtuosic steps, swiftly drawn characterizations, and an astonishing sweep of outlook, movement, and feeling. In all likelihood, no dancer other than Baryshnikov could have performed it effectively.

Still, inevitably, Mikhail Baryshnikov is remembered most conspicuously in the nineteenth-century classics, which offer the roles

PHOTO BY MARTHA SWOPE

Gelsey Kirkland and Mikhail Baryshnikov in the 1978 world premiere of Baryshnikov's *Don Quixote (Kitri's Wedding)*

through which a classical dancer is finally measured. Baryshnikov's virtuosity had, perhaps, its greatest forum in *Don Quixote*, for which he called forth the absolute, stunning clarity of his Kirov training and embellished it with a matador's finesse. Dancing it, he stayed within what he regarded as reasonable boundaries, convinced that something is lost when the piece becomes simply a technical showpiece. His refusal to add extra flash simply because he could was a telling choice born of native restraint and modesty. He always regarded the classical tradition, of which he was an ideal exponent, as more important than his own dancing.

Giselle is the greatest romantic ballet. The contrast between the sunniness of its first act and the pervasive darkness of its second offers the possibility of various interpretative paths. Dancing Albrecht, Baryshnikov settled on a unique shading. Albrecht is often played as a cad, a callous nobleman who harbors no true affection for the lovely peasant girl, Giselle, as he flirts with her, wins her, and finally abandons her, plunging her into madness and death.

Baryshnikov's Albrecht was besotted with the innocent and enchanting Giselle. The tragedy inherent in this rendering derives from Albrecht's need to be near her. Against this charged backdrop, Baryshnikov's dancing had the effect and power of an agonized cry from the heart, one expressed through the perfect double *assemblés* finishing in fourth position, which demonstrated his ability to jump higher and land lower than any danseur.

Some dancers rely on tricks. He had the one trick that matters. His trick was brilliance. And his dancing seemed absent of effort because, ultimately, it derived from some unchartable place where effort is beside the point.

By definition, a classical artist is not concerned with what is new; his concern is what can never grow old. In that sense, and in others, Baryshnikov was not of his time, but of some attenuated moment in time. In an era of self-absorption, his dancing had a selfless quality; in a decade of greed, he personified the power of reduction. In an age of mindless confession, his was the power of containment.

IT MAY BE that Baryshnikov's ideal partner was Gelsey Kirkland, who left New York City Ballet, where she trained and became prominent, to dance with Baryshnikov at Ballet Theatre. Tiny and lithesome, Miss Kirkland had the swiftness, radiance, and idiosyncratic logic of a bit of mercury. For her, ballet steps were the pure distillation of emotion; dancing was an exercise that engaged the

PHOTO BY RICHARD BRAATEN

President Jimmy Carter backstage after the world premiere of Mikhail Baryshnikov's *Don Quixote (Kitri's Wedding)*—left to right: Lucia Chase, Oliver Smith (rear), music director John Lanchbery, Gelsey Kirkland, Baryshnikov, and President Carter (1978)

PHOTO BY JOHN ENGSTEAD

Gelsey Kirkland in Mikhail Baryshnikov's *The Nutracker*, created in 1976

mind. Together, she and Baryshnikov attained a level at which thirty-two *fouettés* or three double *assemblés* are no longer mere steps but a metaphor for the entirety of human potential and striving.

Their most renowned pairings were in Baryshnikov's gifted reworkings of two classics: *The Nutcracker*, the film of which has become the best-selling ballet video, and in *Don Quixote*, whose world premiere, in 1978, was attended by President Jimmy Carter.

The frenzy surrounding that particular event had not been seen in America since Fonteyn and Nureyev's early performances. From the moment Miss Kirkland and Baryshnikov appeared onstage it was apparent that this would be a night on which ballet's consummate artists achieved their utmost. When the evening ended, the audience rose to its feet, cheering, shouting "Bravo!" and "Brava!" and hurling peonies and roses.

In every role, Gelsey Kirkland was capable of transporting the audience. The sort of dancer who comes along but occasionally, her existence substantiated the claim that certain individuals are born to dance. Yet her turbulent soul and harsh insistence on perfection made neither life nor dancing easy for her. She alienated many and drew others in. The choreographer Antony Tudor, a truculent aesthete subject to the same daunting moods and imperatives as she was, was forcefully drawn to her; in Miss Kirkland, he discovered an artist in whom he saw loveliness embodied and his own darkness.

Tudor had not choreographed for ABT in twenty-five years when he returned in 1975 to set his *Shadowplay*, a work created for the Royal Ballet eight years earlier, on Miss Kirkland, Baryshnikov, and Jonas Kage. Miss Kirkland's expressiveness and ethereal suppleness seemed made for his ballets, and he was prompted to create for her a new work, *The Leaves Are Fading*. As his muse, she stirred him to a more fluid, sensuous, and emotionally realized piece than any he had made previously. She went on to perform Caroline in *Jardin Aux Lilas*, with Erik Bruhn appearing as The Man She Must Marry, a role originated by Tudor himself.

Tudor made another ballet for Gelsey Kirkland three years later. *The Tiller in the Fields*, in which he paired her with the towering Patrick Bissell, was a whimsical piece that made use of the way her diminutiveness contrasted with Bissell's size. Like Miss Kirkland, Bissell was an extraordinary artist, whose gifts were exceeded only by his penchant for self-destruction. Standing six foot three, he was uniquely riveting as he took off into the air, which he seemed to own, to embrace, to float on.

He died of a drug overdose in 1987, shortly after Miss Kirkland's accumulated troubles precluded her from dancing. In retrospect, there is something unspeakably poignant about *The Tiller in the Fields*, created as it was on two dancers fated to pass through the ballet world with the brilliance and downward trajectory of shooting stars.

PHOTO BY MARTHA SWOPE

Gelsey Kirkland and Jonas Kage in *The Leaves Are Fading* (1975)

PHOTO BY MARTHA SWOPE

Gelsey Kirkland and Patrick Bissell in *The Tiller in the Fields* (1978)

Among the dancers of the Baryshnikov era were several company members who became established at ABT in the years that Lucia Chase preceded him as artistic director. One was Cynthia Gregory, who joined the company in 1965, stayed on to dance more than seventy ballets, and became one of the most revered and lauded ballerinas in the company's history.

She devoted virtually her entire career to American Ballet Theatre, gathering an astonishingly diverse repertory, which she managed to fashion in her own image, an image that could incorporate every conceivable style. In the classics, she had a dazzling, thoroughbred hauteur and such exceptional stylistic clarity that the critic Clive Barnes likened it to "a textbook written by a lyric poet."

Whatever a role required, she supplied it. As Odette/Odile she was magic and menace personified; her Swanilda was a glistening, merry soubrette; as Myrta, the vengeful Queen of the Wilis, she took on an imperious chill that made her unearthly and unyielding. In romantic roles like the Sylph and Giselle, she softened her outlines, blurring her clarity, dancing with a surpassing grace that was the essence of femininity and poignancy. Her stark rendering of The Accused in *Fall River Legend* delineated the bizarrely isolated quality of one who has drifted into a corner in which societal considerations hold no value. To darkly dramatic works, she brought

PHOTO BY MIRA

Cynthia Gregory in *Swan Lake* (1983)

utter concentration and a sheer intensity of characterization. These qualities could be seen in her portrayal of Medusa in Tudor's darkly psychological *Undertow*, and in Birgit Cullberg's *Miss Julie*, an adaptation of August Strindberg's exploration of the emotional and sexual battle between a noblewoman and her sadistic servant.

She was often partnered by Fernando Bujones, a dancer with consummate technique and eager charm. In the classics, he was a soaring Franz and a tempestuous Romeo; in other works his range extended from the icy Jean in *Miss Julie* to *Fancy Free*'s insouciant, rumba-dancing sailor to the troubled Trangressor in *Undertow*.

Miss Gregory danced with ABT for a total of twenty-seven years. In that time, she never rested on her laurels. Performing, she once remarked, required "putting myself on the line . . . baring my soul every time I go out there." Equally, she never ceased to look for new venues of creativity, even as she remained faithful to the classics. Describing the richness of her gifts, Rudolf Nureyev placed her with the dancers he most admired. "She's capable of being . . . so vulnerable that it becomes terrific . . . the best are like that—giving a kind of love that's totally selfless."

The more her artistry matured, the more it seemed that America itself was reflected in her dancing, which pulsated with the small-town virtues of honesty and lack of pretension and the big-city traits of glamour, wit, and sophistication. It is difficult to imagine a more committed artist. To many, she would never cease to be the quintessential "American" ballerina.

PHOTO BY SUE MARTIN

Cynthia Gregory and Fernando Bujones in *Giselle* (1979)

PHOTO BY MARTHA SWOPE

Cynthia Gregory, Christopher Mattox, and Georgina Parkinson in *Fall River Legend* (1990)

PHOTO BY MARTHA SWOPE

Cynthia Gregory and Fernando Bujones in *Undertow* (1979)

Cynthia Gregory and John Meehan in *Miss Julie* (1979)

Martine van Hamel was a regal dancer, with an absolute directness and absence of guile that lent her an abundance of that inexplicable quality known as "presence." Throughout her twenty-one years at ABT, she melded with each role she danced, so much so that audiences seeing such long familiar characters as Odette/Odile in *Swan Lake*, Aurora in *The Sleeping Beauty*, and Myrta in *Giselle* saw them more deeply and clearly when Miss van Hamel danced them. To see her in a particular work was to see a definitive performance that prompted audiences to retain a picture of her dancing that part, regardless of who else you saw in it.

Her work was deepened by a generosity that manifested as a stunning expansiveness of spirit and gesture. Imbued with the artist's desire to become whatever role she played, she was blessed with the imaginative empathy to achieve that aim. Her doomed Desdemona in José Limón's *The Moor's Pavane* was heartrendingly pure and trusting. In the lead ballerina role in Twyla Tharp's *Push Comes to Shove*, a role created for her, she was chic and sophistication personified. The title role in Glen Tetley's *Sphinx*, also created for her, called upon her focus, *plastique*, and sense of drama. In that work, Miss van Hamel was partnered by Clark Tippet, who took the role of Oedipus, enhancing it with his uncommon partnering skills and the deep intelligence he brought to performing. Another of her frequent partners was Patrick Bissell, her equal in technique and verve, presence and size. Their dancing captured the particular luminosity that comes from the blending of two extraordinary dancers.

Becoming a ballet dancer, Miss van Hamel was convinced, was notably less difficult than remaining one. With that in mind, she insisted upon remaining a student long after she had become a ballet star with impeccable technique and a range that astounded audiences. She never ceased improving. When she gave a performance that met her standards, she sought to learn from it, to dissect its dynamics in order to repeat them, though she was aware that it is not easy to re-create magic. "It's elusive," she noted, "especially in the classics."

PHOTO BY MARTHA SWOPE

The Moor's Pavane with (left to right) Sallie Wilson, Ivan Nagy, Erik Bruhn, and Martine van Hamel (1977)

PHOTO BY MARTHA SWOPE

Martine van Hamel and Clark Tippet in *Sphinx* (1977)

PHOTO BY RICHARD N. GREENHOUSE

Martine van Hamel and Patrick Bissell in Natalia Makarova's 1983 staging of *Paquita*

PHOTO BY MARTHA SWOPE

Etudes with (left to right) Ross Stretton, Martine van Hamel, and Kevin McKenzie (1987)

PHOTO BY SUE MARTIN

Martine van Hamel and Kevin McKenzie in *Torso* (1982)

Yet in classical works she was bewitching, at times imposing, at other times exuberant, her profound musicality informing each move she made. She would have had it no other way; interpreting the music, she believed, was as vital to a performance as interpreting the role.

In Nureyev's *Raymonda* and later in the divertissements Baryshnikov staged from the ballet, she had the sparkle and sharpness of a multifaceted diamond. She glowed in the bravura ballerina role in Harold Lander's *Études*. Whatever she danced, she always seemed elated to be performing. Miss van Hamel often danced with Kevin McKenzie, who was also her partner offstage. Both could imbue their work with a meditative quality; their physiques and beings seemed matched, like halves of a single coin. Dancing together, they extracted from one another a striking intensity.

When Kevin McKenzie arrived at Ballet Theatre in 1979, his clean, flowing technique and princely grace established him in the finest *danseur noble* tradition. As a consequence he was uniquely qualified for leading romantic roles in a wide variety of works and so was required to learn a great deal in little time. He gave his first performances of *Jardin Aux Lilas* and Act II of *La Bayadère* on the same night. The next day he debuted as Siegfried in *Swan Lake;* two months later, he performed his first *Giselle* and first full-length *La Bayadère*.

His work was an arresting blend of litheness and seriousness, by turns filled with poetry and breezy exuberance. In each role, he demonstrated a technical brilliance that set him apart from other American *premier danseurs*. His impressively soaring technique enhanced his portrayal of Solor, and his exceptional partnering

PHOTO BY MIRA

Kevin McKenzie in *Swan Lake* (1984)

PHOTO BY MIRA

Natalia Makarova and Kevin McKenzie in *Romeo and Juliet* (1985)

skills and emotional amplitude made him one of the most courtly and prized of Romeos.

He was also an unusually thoughtful performer capable of apprehending the most minute and the largest outlines of a given part. Dancing Solor, Her Lover, Prince Siegfried, and Albrecht he detected, in these roles, a common thread, which was that each of these characters is forever changed by a single event.

To make real the depths of emotion such stunning events engender, he determined to draw upon his experience, though by his own account, that experience was limited. He had never wanted to be anything other than a ballet dancer. Ballet had fixed his life's breadth and boundaries; his dedication to it was unequivocal. Yet he would never dance comprehensively, he decided, unless he lived comprehensively, a conviction that provided a watershed for him and ultimately allowed him to steep his performances in emotional actuality.

A romantic dancer, he had a curiosity and daring that prompted him to revel in dancing works opposed to his essential type. He was vibrant in Jerome Robbins's *Fancy Free*; in Agnes de Mille's *Rodeo* he was a notable Champion Roper. Yet his ardent manner and flawlessly smooth dancing made the classics his perfect vehicle.

McKenzie was a gallant and masterful partner who enhanced

Marianna Tcherkassky and Kevin McKenzie in *Giselle* (1985)

many ballerinas, among them the ethereal Marianna Tcherkassky, a romantic ballerina of Japanese and Russian parentage. Miss Tcherkassky was small and delicate, a child-woman with exceptionally supple limbs and intense, dark eyes. Her buoyancy, lovely technique, and profound sense of drama earned her the distinction of being regarded as one of the outstanding Giselles. Upon seeing Sir Kenneth MacMillan's *Romeo and Juliet* performed by the Royal Ballet, she was filled with longing to dance Juliet and her portrayal of that role became one of the brightest spots in a career that always had a particular luster. It was fitting that she danced it on the poignant, early summer evening when she gave her farewell performance.

In 1980, when Mikhail Baryshnikov became artistic director of American Ballet Theatre, the company was still operating as it had from its inception, supplementing its own cadre of dancers with ballet stars imported with considerable fanfare for particular seasons or occasions. This practice was beneficial for ticket sales but disheartening for dancers, given that it dimmed their own prospects for advancement into coveted principal parts. This changed with Baryshnikov, whose stated intention was to make "the star" the company itself.

From the start, it was clear that he would expect of other dancers the same scrupulous professionalism he demanded of himself. Even on the night he defected, he dutifully arrived at the O'Keefe Center in Toronto before abandoning the Kirov Ballet during its engagement there. "It wouldn't be right to leave," he thought at the time, "without first doing the performance."

He consequently had scant sympathy for, or patience with, the demands of stars whose concern, he believed, was for their own future rather than for the company. "It's all what they can do and what they can't do and when and with whom," he said, venting his annoyance some years later. "All these people had their problems."

He wanted to create his own stars. As a signal of that desire, upon his arrival at ABT, he hired an unknown dancer as a principal. Magali Messac, previously of the Pennsylvania Ballet, was a particularly lovely ballerina on whom he later created his *Cinderella*. Yet he would not entirely avoid established dancers, and brought several in at various points. Most were from the Soviet Union, as was Alexander Godunov, Baryshnikov's classmate at ballet school in Latvia, who had become a Soviet defector and a surpassingly glamorous and forceful danseur.

For the most part, however, Baryshnikov instituted a system generally used at the New York City Ballet, the company founded and directed by the man of dance he most revered, George Balanchine, who had left the Soviet Union in search of the expanded artistic opportunities that Baryshnikov came seeking fifty years later. Under this system, a company seeks to develop its own stars by encouraging gifted young dancers to ascend over time from the corps de ballet to soloist, then, perhaps, on to principal dancer. This meant that each young dancer's potential would be regarded seriously, as Baryshnikov demonstrated on the opening night of his inaugural season as artistic director when he cast the female role in "Pas d'Esclave," a pas de deux from *Le Corsaire*. The male role was to be danced by Godunov. As his partner, Baryshnikov chose an eighteen-year-old from the corps de ballet named Susan Jaffe. So began the process through which Miss Jaffe developed into one of the company's most beloved ballerinas.

When ABT's dancers realized that their efforts would be noticed and rewarded, the general level of dancing was transformed, as the corps de ballet began to perform as if each onstage moment were an audition and soloists pushed themselves as far as talent and will could take them. ABT had become a meritocracy and, in a sense, a

PHOTO BY MARTHA SWOPE

Susan Jaffe, in her first performance with ABT, dances "Pas d'Esclave" from *Le Corsaire* with Alexander Godunov (1980)

Darwinian system in which the fittest did not merely survive, but could establish themselves, as Miss Jaffe did, in the first rank of the company.

In the early 1980s, Baryshnikov promoted six gifted soloists to the rank of principal dancer. One was Victor Barbee, who seemed literally to alter in physical size as he subsumed himself with each successive characterization. Whether as Tybalt in *Romeo and Juliet* or as the High Brahmin in *La Bayadère*, his work captured every conceivable nuance and evinced the great emotional scope that can be portrayed on a ballet stage. Over the years, he would enhance countless ABT productions with his original and profoundly empathetic imagination. "You don't have to know what the character's going to do," he told other dancers when he later became a ballet master, "you just have to know what they feel."

Michael Owen, another exceptional character dancer, brought a distinct maturity to the stage with his meticulously drawn portrayals. Playing Von Rotbart in Baryshnikov's *Swan Lake*, his face obscured by a mask, he was forced to rely solely on his body and the movement to attain the requisite evil intensity. His daunting range allowed him to be equally convincing as the gleefully wicked Carabosse in *The Sleeping Beauty*, as the overbearing Lord Capulet in *Romeo and Juliet*, and as the compassionate friend in Tudor's *Pillar of Fire*.

Then there was Danilo Radojevic, who decided upon his profession at age seven, when his mother took him to see Nureyev dance. His vigor and insouciance made a charming combination that led to his selection as Baryshnikov's replacement in *Push Comes to Shove*. He danced many roles at ABT, from Prince Florimund to

PHOTO BY MARTHA SWOPE

Kenneth MacMillan rehearsing *Romeo and Juliet* with (left to right) Victor Barbee, Danilo Radojevic, Robert La Fosse, and Ross Stretton (1985)

the Prince in Baryshnikov's *Cinderella,* but his most memorable role may be Mercutio in *Romeo and Juliet,* for which he allied his bravura technique with the persona of a quixotic urchin.

Ross Stretton was an anomaly in a profession for which training usually begins at age five or six. Stretton was working as an auto mechanic in his hometown of Canberra, Australia, when he saw a ballet company perform. One of the men had an amazing jump; watching him, Stretton decided to go to Melbourne and become a ballet dancer. He was eighteen, the age at which training is normally completed. Still, he went on to dance with the Australian Ballet and the Joffrey prior to joining ABT as a soloist in 1981. Two years later, he was promoted to principal dancer. Eventually he became a director of the company and later, artistic director of the Australian Ballet.

A very special dancer was Leslie Browne, who joined ABT as a soloist in 1976 and became a principal dancer ten years later. The daughter of former ABT dancers Kelly Brown and Isabel Mirrow, whose story was told in *The Turning Point,* both she and her gifted brother, Ethan, who joined the company in 1981, seemed fated to be ABT dancers. Deeply expressive, Miss Browne's dancing could be profoundly affecting. As Myrta, Queen of the Wilis, she was implacable, a fearsome figure with fixed eyes, set upon revenge. In romantic roles like Juliet, she was enchantingly pliant. A leading interpreter of Tudor ballets, she especially loved *Pillar of Fire.* The ballet was so well constructed, she later observed, that each shape of the movement told the dancer precisely what the emotion should be.

Her dramatic abilities led to roles in three movies: *Nijinsky, Dancers,* and *The Turning Point,* in which, playing the daughter of the character based on her mother and played by Shirley MacLaine, she literally played herself.

Cynthia Harvey joined ABT's corps de ballet in 1974. In the next eight years she advanced from soloist to principal dancer. She took a two-year leave to dance with the Royal Ballet, where she was the first American ballerina to be a company member. Driven to constantly improve, she loved working in the studio, and viewed each role she danced as a means of broadening her understanding of herself, of women, of life. Her career had many high points, including her first *Swan Lake* with Baryshnikov and her first *Don Quixote* with Anthony Dowell, an occasion on which the audience erupted in "Bravos!" and pelted them with flowers. Her career was grounded in her capacity for hard work; reviewing all the fine attributes of her dancing, she found that she was proudest of that.

During his years at ABT, Baryshnikov promoted several members of the corps de ballet to soloist and then to principal dancer. Cheryl Yeager joined the corps in 1976, became a soloist in 1981, and a principal dancer six years later. Her performances were imbued with style, musicality, and an appetite for adventure that gave her dancing an extra excitement. As *The Sleeping Beauty*'s Aurora she brimmed with the vivacity of a young girl on the cusp of womanhood; as *Don Quixote*'s Kitri she evinced the boundless spirit of a character intended to be the most vibrant woman on the planet. She always gave an impression of effortlessness, whether flying through the air as Kitri, or supplying the fleetness required for Bournonville's *Flower Festival in Genzano.*

Miss Yeager had great respect for her profession: the day she was promoted to principal dancer, she would say, was the happiest day of her life. Another significant moment was the night she danced *La Sylphide* with Erik Bruhn as Madge and Baryshnikov as James. She felt honored to take her curtain call standing between them.

Robert La Fosse, who joined ABT in 1977, was made a principal dancer six years later. His boyish charm, buoyant personality, and immense dedication soon drew attention. He excelled in emotionally and technically diverse ballets. As the Prodigal Son, his performance was wrenching; as the sailor in *Fancy Free,* he was ebullient.

Finally, there was Johan Renvall, who grew up in Stockholm, where he was a junior ice-skating champion. The skater's taste for speed, form, and daring were useful to a young man who would become a virtuoso dancer. He came to ABT in 1978 and was promoted to principal dancer nine years later. His sharp and bright technique, with its perfectly articulated movements, made him memorable in a variety of roles, chief among them his rowdy Mercutio and his exquisitely stylized Bronze Idol.

ARTISTIC DIRECTORS imprint themselves on a company as surely as a hot iron imprints on cloth. In choosing works for ABT, Baryshnikov's selections and commissions were the choices of an artist whose hunger for new repertory sprang from the prodigious curiosity, artistic ambition, and restlessness at the core of his defection.

Central among the works he presented were nineteenth-century classics, all of which manifested his knowledge of ballet tradition and of the choreographers and dancers most responsible for elevating it. For instance, in 1983 he commissioned Natalia Makarova to stage a revival of *Paquita,* originally choreographed by Joseph Mazilier in Paris and later staged in St. Petersburg by Petipa, the peerless nineteenth-century choreographer. A rarely seen classical work, *Paquita*'s grand pas de deux entered Ballet Theatre's repertory in 1957 when it was danced by Nora Kaye and Erik Bruhn. In 1971, Nureyev mounted his own version on the company, giving the leading roles to Cynthia Gregory and Michaël Denard. In Makarova's production, Martine van Hamel and Kevin McKenzie danced the roles performed in the 1846 Mazilier original by the legendary Lucien Petipa and Carlotta Grisi, the ballerina for whom *Giselle*

PHOTO BY MARTHA SWOPE

Cheryl Yeager and Peter Fonseca in the pas de deux from *Flower Festival in Genzano* (1983)

was made, and its original Albrecht. *Paquita* represented an encapsulation of one hundred and fifty years of ballet, a heritage passed down and reworked but kept within the unwavering perimeters of classicism.

Baryshnikov also commissioned many contemporary works by choreographers he perceived as significant and intriguing. Some were created for the choreographer's own company, as in the case of pieces by Eliot Feld, Martha Graham, Paul Taylor, Merce Cunningham, and the more classical Jiri Kylian. Others were created for ABT. But each reflects Baryshnikov's artistic daring and are generally of interest, even when they were not well received.

BARYSHNIKOV'S TENURE, and the 1980s, commenced with Brian Shaw's revival of Sir Frederick Ashton's early work *Les Rendezvous,* an enchanting confection to music by Auber and originally created for Alicia Markova and Stanislas Idzikowski.

Baryshnikov's regard for the classics led him to August Bournonville, the leading Danish choreographer of the nineteenth century, whose exquisite works instituted the Royal Danish Ballet's tradition of restrained elegance, airborne lightness, and exceptionally swift footwork. Bournonville's emphasis on the male role in dancing gave rise to the Royal Danish Ballet's tradition of creating superlative male dancers, of whom Erik Bruhn was the most exemplary. The Bournonville school also produced Stanley Williams, one of the Royal Danish Ballet's extraordinary danseurs, who went on to become cochairman of the faculty at the School of American Ballet, where he became ballet's most lauded and influential teacher.

Baryshnikov often took class with Williams, and in 1982 asked him to stage the pas de deux from Bournonville's charming *Flower Festival in Genzano*, a ballet originally created in 1858 and last danced for ABT in the 1960s by Carla Fracci and Erik Bruhn.

A second restaging was the most cherished of Bournonville ballets, the enchanting and mystical *La Sylphide*, a work created

PHOTO BY MARTHA SWOPE

Airs with (left to right) Anna Spelman, Lisa Rinehart, Brian Adams, and Johan Renvall (1983)

PHOTO BY JACK BUXBAUM

Susan Jaffe and Mikhail Baryshnikov in *Variations on "America"* (1982)

PHOTO BY MARTHA SWOPE

Marianna Tcherkassky in *Les Rendezvous* (1980)

in 1836 when the leading male role was danced by the choreographer. Baryshnikov first saw ABT's version of it when the company was on tour in the Soviet Union. On that occasion, the Sylph was danced by Toni Lander, an ABT ballerina trained at the Royal Danish Ballet, while Royes Fernandez danced James, the young Scotsman who falls in love with her. Captivated, Baryshnikov asked to dance the role of James immediately upon his arrival in the West. Erik Bruhn coached him, offering meticulous corrections and thus schooling Baryshnikov in a wholly new and demanding style renowned for its unusual number of jumps and beats.

In 1983, Baryshnikov asked Bruhn to stage *La Sylphide*. The opening night cast included Marianna Tcherkassky and Fernando Bujones, with Bruhn forsaking his career as a *danseur noble* by taking on the character role of Madge, the evil witch.

Of the classical works performed during his directorship, many were staged by Baryshnikov himself. His *Cinderella*, created with Peter Anastos, was distinguished by quirky humor and a profound sense of classical style. Other stagings were based on the Petipa works, which form the basis of classicism in general and the repertory of the Kirov in particular. Each of these ballets has distinct features that Baryshnikov both incorporated and expanded upon. His staging of *The Nutcracker* had an otherworldly quality and

PHOTO BY MARTHA SWOPE

Erik Bruhn coaching Mikhail Baryshnikov and Cheryl Yeager in *La Sylphide* (1983)

PHOTO BY MARTHA SWOPE

Marianna Tcherkassky and Fernando Bujones in *La Sylphide* (1983)

PHOTO BY MARTHA SWOPE

Mikhail Baryshnikov rehearses Gil Boggs and Marianna Tcherkassky in *Cinderella* (1983)

PHOTO BY MARTHA SWOPE

Patrick Bissell as the Prince, with (left to right) Robert La Fosse and Victor Barbee as the Stepsisters in Mikhail Baryshnikov's *Cinderella* (1983)

PHOTO BY MARTHA SWOPE

Marianna Tcherkassky and Alexander Minz rehearsing Mikhail Baryshnikov's *The Nutcracker* (1976)

included a heavenly pas de deux imbued with the uncommon beauty and lightness of a snowflake. His *Don Quixote* was stocked with raw energy, rustic humor, and exuberant virtuosity. His *Swan Lake* took a novel approach to the 1895 classic. His lavish stagings of the divertissements from *Raymonda* were popular repertory items.

In 1985, Baryshnikov commissioned the first of two story ballets from Sir Kenneth MacMillan, who succeeded Ashton as director of the Royal Ballet and went on to be regarded as among the foremost contemporary creators of full-length classical works. Baryshnikov formalized MacMillan's role with ABT by giving him the title of associate artistic director.

MacMillan had created his *Romeo and Juliet* in 1965 on two Royal Ballet dancers of his own choosing who, as his muses, substantially influenced the title parts. Lynn Seymour imparted her own headstrong, impassioned nature to Juliet, while the tall, handsome Christopher Gable's youth and naturalness gave Romeo an innocence and dreaminess. These were such wonderful roles that, prior to the world premiere, they were usurped by the undisputed stars of the Royal Ballet, Fonteyn and Nureyev, who filtered everything they danced through their own particular stage personas. Fonteyn's Juliet was demure until Romeo ignites her. Nureyev's Romeo was a madly flirtatious boy who happens upon genuine

PHOTO BY MARTHA SWOPE

Cynthia Gregory and Fernando Bujones in Mikhail Baryshnikov's *Raymonda* (Divertissements from Act II and Act III) in 1980

PHOTO BY MARTHA SWOPE

Kenneth MacMillan's *Romeo and Juliet* with (left to right) Wes Chapman as Benvolio, Robert La Fosse as Romeo, Danilo Radojevic as Mercutio, and Susan Jones as the Nurse (1985)

passion and seriousness with Juliet. The ballet provided Fonteyn and Nureyev with one of their partnership's greatest successes, and their interpretations persist in most subsequent productions, despite the fact that they were not quite what the choreographer envisioned.

At ABT, *Romeo and Juliet* premiered in 1985, with Leslie Browne and Robert La Fosse giving the title roles dramatic and rhapsodic fervor. They were coached by ABT's ballet mistress Georgina Parkinson, a close friend of MacMillan and a former Royal Ballet dancer who played the lovely Rosaline in the original production and was later a notable Juliet. Mercutio was danced by Danilo Radojevic, while the role of Benvolio brought to prominence a young dancer who had recently joined the company, Wes Chapman. The mime roles of Escalus and Friar Laurence were taken by John Taras, a choreographer who had worked with Balanchine for many years, and whom Baryshnikov had hired as his associate director. In later performances, these roles were perfectly portrayed by David Richardson, an ABT ballet master who went on to be assistant artistic director.

MacMillan also staged Petipa's *The Sleeping Beauty*, the tale of the hexed and slumbering princess awakened by a kiss. Mounted on the company in 1987, this was a brightening of the Royal Ballet's traditional version with a few individual touches and lavish new designs by Nicholas Georgiadis.

MacMillan's *Anastasia*, to music by Peter Ilyitch Tchaikovsky and Bohuslav Martinu, depicted Anna Anderson, the putative Anastasia as a young girl in Russia's imperial court and, in a mental hospital at her life's end and reflected MacMillan's fascination with early-twentieth-century history. The work began as a single act, created for the Berlin Ballet. Later, that piece became the third act of

PHOTO BY MARTHA SWOPE

Michael Owen as Carabosse in Kenneth MacMillan's *The Sleeping Beauty* (1987)

PHOTO BY PETE MCARTHUR

Anastasia, Act II (1985), with Cynthia Gregory and Clark Tippet

PHOTO BY MARTHA SWOPE

Mikhail Baryshnikov in *The Wild Boy* (1981)

the full-evening *Anastasia* MacMillan created for the Royal Ballet, which Ballet Theatre revived for the 1999 spring season.

In his years as artistic associate, MacMillan made only two new ballets for the company. The first, *The Wild Boy*, was loosely based on Francois Truffaut's 1969 film, *The Wild Child*, and dealt with the divide between primitive innocence and sophisticated decadence. The other was *Requiem*, a strange ballet with music that Andrew Lloyd Weber composed soon after his father's death. The ballet's underlying theme was inspired by another event: the conflict of a young Cambodian boy given the choice between killing his sister and saving himself. The leading role was created on Baryshnikov, but danced at the world premiere by Gil Boggs. It became one of the first ABT performances of Alessandra Ferri, who had worked with MacMillan at the Royal Ballet, where she became a leading interpreter of his work.

Baryshnikov was determined to bring new contemporary works to the repertory. In the past, such pieces had been introduced for the pleasure and interest of the audience. Baryshnikov had a further motive. Believing that contemporary pieces embellish a dancer's stagecraft and technique in the classics, he brought them to the company for the dancers.

ABT had three works by Jerome Robbins: *Fancy Free*, created for the company in 1944, *Les Noces*, choreographed in 1965, and *Other Dances*. In 1982, a Robbins piece crafted for Jerome Robbins Ballets and first danced at the 1958 Festival of Two Worlds in Spoleto, Italy, was added to the repertory. *N.Y. Export: Op. Jazz* was a formal, abstract ballet that featured finger-snapping, ponytailed, sneaker-wearing dancers. Energized and alienated, they embodied youth in the 1950s.

The most innovative aspect of Baryshnikov's tenure at ABT was the introduction of Twyla Tharp, a modern-dance choreographer, as one of his two artistic associates. Tharp's original, disjointed

PHOTO BY MARTHA SWOPE

Requiem (1986) with (left to right) Clark Tippet, Robert Hill, Alessandra Ferri, and Ross Stretton

PHOTO BY MARTY SOHL

Requiem with Alessandra Ferri and Mikhail Baryshnikov (1986)

Other Dances with Alessandra Ferri and Julio Bocca (1991)

PHOTO BY MIRA

N.Y. *Export: Op. Jazz*, staged for ABT in 1982

PHOTO BY MARTHA SWOPE

takes on ballet steps, first demonstrated in *Push Comes to Shove,* provided the repertory with a new way of approaching the classic vocabulary. Year after year, she added new pieces that demonstrated her arresting blend of ballet and jazz, modern and classical, lyrical and deconstructed movement.

The charming *The Little Ballet* utilized the well-known Glazunov score for *Scènes de Ballet;* there were also the fluid *Sinatra Suite,* the balletic *Quartet,* and *Bach Partita,* a full-company work that Tharp later regarded as having helped to consolidate her position with the company. Each work revealed a novel approach to steps, to music, and to the ways they intertwine.

This was especially true of *In the Upper Room,* which ABT presented in 1988. An immensely popular work to music by Phillip Glass, it was created for Tharp's own company two years earlier. Tharp invariably made interesting use of dancers, creating difficult and unexpected parts for them that used their gifts and stage personalities in new and arresting ways. For example, *Brief Fling,* an exceptionally brilliant piece and Baryshnikov's last Tharp commission for ABT, had a stunning and taxing role for a seemingly effortless Julio Bocca.

Another choreographer Baryshnikov respected and honored was Antony Tudor, to whom he gave the title choreographer emeritus. Reviving four of his works, he sought to make Tudor happy; his efforts in that regard may have taught him that this was no simple task.

PHOTO BY MARTHA SWOPE

Deirdre Carberry and Mikhail Baryshnikov in *The Little Ballet* (1983)

PHOTO BY MARTHA SWOPE

Elaine Kudo and Mikhail Baryshnikov in *Sinatra Suite* (1984)

PHOTO BY MARTHA SWOPE

Bach Partita (1983) with (left to right) Robert La Fosse, Magali Messac, Cynthia Gregory, Fernando Bujones, Martine van Hamel, and Clark Tippet

PHOTO © 1985 JACK MITCHELL

Dim Lustre, revived in 1985 with Leslie Browne and John Meehan

Jardin Aux Lilas, created for London's Ballet Rambert in 1936, is the supreme choreographic evocation of love never to be. It had premiered at ABT in 1940 with Viola Essen as Caroline, Hugh Laing as Her Lover, and Tudor as The Man She Must Marry. In a notable production four decades later, with Gelsey Kirkland as Caroline and Erik Bruhn in the role Tudor originated, it was apparent that this great work, like all works of its caliber, was a vehicle for truths that are ageless and undying.

Gala Performance, created for Tudor's London Ballet in 1938, was first performed at ABT three years later, with a cast that included Nora Kaye as La Reine de la Danse.This fragile burlesque portrayed three competing ballerinas, Russian, Italian, and French, each of whom presents her particular style to a doting public.

Dim Lustre was created for Ballet Theatre in 1943, with Nora Kaye dancing The Lady with Him and Hugh Laing as The Gentleman with Her. The revival was danced by Leslie Browne and John Meehan, who captured just the right note for the separate pasts of a feuding couple. Its theme of Proustian remembrance was one of Tudor's preoccupations.

The final Tudor work was *Fandango*, which had been created for students in 1963 and demonstrated Tudor's absolute mastery of choreographic construction.

PHOTO BY MARTY SOHL

The 1987 restaging of *Gala Performance* with Leslie Browne, Susan Jaffe, and Alessandra Ferri

Of all the choreographers with whom Baryshnikov worked, Balanchine held special meaning for him in part because his works were among the few that he found challenging. *Theme and Variations* was, he insisted, the most difficult ballet he had danced since arriving in the West.

Balanchine created *Apollo* in 1928 for Diaghilev's Ballet Russes, with Serge Lifar as Apollo. He gave the ballet to Ballet Theatre in 1943, six years before his City Ballet was established. At that time, Apollo was danced by André Eglevsky, with Balanchine's wife, Vera Zorina, as Terpsichore.

This was the full *Apollo*, a version different from the one eventually danced at City Ballet. Commencing with Apollo's birth, it ends when the young god hears his father's call and ascends, with his muses, toward heaven. In 1974, Eglevsky restaged this version of the ballet for ABT. An unparalleled neoclassic work, with a momentous Stravinsky score, it was performed over the years, providing each danseur cast as Apollo with a meaningful rite of passage.

In nearly every year of his directorship, Baryshnikov introduced a new Balanchine ballet into the repertory, in the process demonstrating the choreographer's uncanny stylistic reach:

PHOTO BY RICHARD N. GREENHOUSE

Apollo with (left to right) Christine Spizzo, Cheryl Yeager, Susan Jaffe, and Mikhail Baryshnikov (1983)

PHOTO BY MARTHA SWOPE

Cynthia Gregory and Robert La Fosse in *Prodigal Son* (1980)

PHOTO BY MARTHA SWOPE

Bourrée Fantasque (1981)

PHOTO BY RICHARD N. GREENHOUSE

Symphonie Concertante (1983)

there was the biblical force and fierce virtuosity of *The Prodigal Son;* the haunting poetry and eerie delicacy of *La Sonnambula,* which portrays women as beyond the essential reach of men and man's fascination with them as fatal; there was *Bourrée Fantasque* with its romantic pas de deux sandwiched between satirical renderings of dance; and there was the unfettered buoyancy of the *Harlequinade* pas de deux.

In 1983, Baryshnikov brought into ABT's repertory *Symphonie Concertante,* which had gone unperformed at City Ballet for nearly thirty years. One of Balanchine's rare works to Mozart, it was a demonstration of the relationship between dance and music. The following year, there was the sprightly *Donizetti Variations;* next came the striking purity of *Stravinsky Violin Concerto.* Finally, Baryshnikov introduced Balanchine's stately *Ballet Imperial,* an ode to Czarist Russia.

Baryshnikov also made use of the works of Agnes de Mille, who, as previously noted, brought a rich strain of Americana to American Ballet Theatre and whose early works, like *Tally Ho* and *Three Virgins and a Devil,* made her a forceful element in the company's self-definition. Her *Rodeo,* created for the Ballet Russe de Monte

PHOTO BY MARTHA SWOPE

Ballet Imperial (1988) with Susan Jaffe and Ross Stretton

Carlo and revived by ABT in 1950 and again at the end of the Baryshnikov years, was a classic American romance in which a spirited girl gets her man.

De Mille's work in a somber vein could be seen in *Fall River Legend* and *The Other,* which depicted the romantic triangle most familiar in her works, that between The Maiden, The Lover, and The Other. But it was on view most strikingly in *The Informer,* a ballet loosely based on dances she created for *Juno,* the Broadway musical based on the Sean O'Casey play *Juno and the Paycock. The Informer* drew an intense picture of Ireland during the Troubles, and was graced by the vivid dramatic performances of Kathleen Moore, Johan Renvall, and Victor Barbee.

PHOTO BY ANTHONY CRICKMAY

Rodeo with Kathleen Moore and John Gardner (1990)

PHOTO BY RICHARD N. GREENHOUSE

The Other (1992) with Amanda McKerrow, Victor Barbee, and Roger van Fleteren

PHOTO BY MARTHA SWOPE

Bruch Violin Concerto No. 1 (1987)

PHOTO BY MARTHA SWOPE

Amanda McKerrow and John Gardner in *Some Assembly Required* (1989)

PHOTO BY MARTY SOHL

Amy Rose and Mikhail Baryshnikov in *Murder* (1986)

One of the few choreographers to emerge from the company was Clark Tippet, a much-loved dancer with an eye for the crisp and grand steps that imbue classicism. Of the several works he created before his early death, his musical visualization *Bruch Violin Concerto No. 1* and his temperamental duet *Some Assembly Required* have found enduring places in the company's repertory.

Baryshnikov also experimented with postmodern choreography, notably in David Gordon's charadelike *Murder* and the equally obscure *The Mollino Room* by Karole Armitage. The latter had vivid decor by David Salle, and while both had arresting facets, neither gained much approval from critics or audiences.

A work that remained in ABT's repertory was Mark Morris's *Drink to Me Only with Thine Eyes*, a lyrical ballet to a piano score by Virgil Thomson. This was a particularly entrancing piece by a choreographer known for his musicality and idiosyncratic manner. Morris's rehearsals were events unto themselves. Years later, dancers would recall him in the rehearsal studio, sipping from a can of Foster's beer as the day's work proceeded.

During the company's early years, one of Diaghilev's choreographers held a place of considerable significance. He was Leonide Massine, known to present-day audiences as the Shoemaker in *The Red Shoes*. In 1988, Baryshnikov invited his son, Lorca Massine, to produce a version of his father's *Gaîté Parisienne*, which had premiered with the Ballet Russe de Monte Carlo fifty years earlier. For this production, sensational new costumes were supplied by the couturier Christian Lacroix. *Gaîté* was a frothy champagne bubble of a work, a bright evocation of turn-of-the-century Paris culminating in a cancan.

PHOTO BY MARTHA SWOPE

Final dress rehearsal for *Drink to Me Only with Thine Eyes* (1988) with (left to right) Susan Jaffe, Martine van Hamel, Mikhail Baryshnikov, choreographer Mark Morris, and (stooping) designer Santo Loquasto

PHOTO BY MARTHA SWOPE

Mikhail Baryshnikov, Leslie Browne, and Ricardo Bustamante in *The Mollino Room* (1986)

PHOTO BY MARTHA SWOPE

Drink to Me Only with Thine Eyes with (left to right) Mikhail Baryshnikov, Kathleen Moore, Carld Jonaissant, Susan Jaffe, Robert Hill, Martine van Hamel, Julio Bocca, and Isabella Padovani (1988)

PHOTO BY MARTHA SWOPE

Gaîté Parisienne with (left to right) Michael Owen, Johan Renvall, Susan Jaffe, Victor Barbee, and John Gardner (1988)

PHOTO BY MARTY SOHL

In the Upper Room (1988)

PHOTO BY MIRA

Alessandra Ferri and Julio Bocca in *Other Dances* (1991)

Nina Ananiashvili in *The Sleeping Beauty*, Act III (1998)

PHOTO BY NANCY ELLISON

PHOTO BY MIRA

Wes Chapman and Amanda McKerrow in *Ballet Imperial* (1988)

PHOTO BY MIRA

Alessandra Ferri as The Accused in *Fall River Legend* (1992)

PHOTO BY MARTHA SWOPE

Fall River Legend (1992)

Swan Lake, Act I

PHOTO BY MIRA

Amanda McKerrow and Robert Hill in *Manon*, Act II (1993)

PHOTO BY MIRA

PHOTO BY ROY ROUND

Keith Roberts in *The Rite of Spring* (1992)

PHOTO BY JANN WHALEY

The Snow Maiden, Act III

PHOTO BY MIRA

Le Corsaire, Act I

PHOTO BY PAUL KOLNIK

The Sleeping Beauty, Act II with Julie Kent and Guillaume Graffin (1997)

Rodeo (1989)

Cynthia Harvey in *Don Quixote*, Act I (1991)

PHOTO BY NANCY ELLISON

Victor Barbee and Ethan Stiefel in *Coppélia* (1998)

PHOTO BY MARTHA SWOPE

Echoing of Trumpets (1994)

PHOTO BY MARTHA SWOPE

Firebird (1992)

PHOTO BY HIDEMI SETO

Susan Jaffe and Jose Manuel Carreño in *Swan Lake*, Act III (1992)

PHOTO BY MARTHA SWOPE

Kathleen Moore in *The Red Shoes* (1994)

PHOTO BY MIRA

Paloma Herrera in *Don Quixote*, Act I (1995)

PHOTO BY NANCY ELLISON

Michael Owen as Madge in *La Sylphide* (1998)

Chez Maxim's, *The Merry Widow,* Act III (1997)

PHOTO BY PAUL KOLNIK

PHOTO BY PAUL KOLNIK

Remanso (left to right) Desmond Richardson, Vladimir Malakhov, Parrish Maynard (1997)

PHOTO BY MARTHA SWOPE

The Nutcracker, Act II (McKenzie production) in 1993

PHOTO BY MIRA

Ashley Tuttle in *Cinderella* (1996)

PHOTO BY MIRA

Ethan Stiefel, *Le Corsaire* (1998)

PHOTO BY MARTHA SWOPE

Kevin McKenzie choreographing his version of *The Nutcracker* (1993)

PHOTO BY MARTHA SWOPE

Birthday Offering (1990)

Chapter Three

THE McKENZIE ERA

As the 1980s had begun with Ashton's *Les Rendezvous*, so the 1990s would commence with Ashton's alluring *Birthday Offering*. Created in 1956 to mark the twenty-fifth anniversary of the Royal Ballet, this lovely, flowing piece with variations for seven ballerinas was danced in honor of American Ballet Theatre's fiftieth anniversary. ABT's dancers had the rare privilege of being coached by Ashton's favorite ballerina, Dame Margot Fonteyn, who had taken the leading ballerina role in the original production. Her part was danced by Susan Jaffe, who was partnered by Ross Stretton, in one of his final performances.

By the time *Birthday Offering* was given on the Metropolitan Opera House's stage during the ABT spring season of 1990, Baryshnikov had vacated his post at the company, leaving the artistic directorship to two individuals whose association with ABT was profound and lengthy. They were the Met's former presentations director, Jane Hermann, and Oliver Smith, the renowned set designer and ABT's codirector, with Lucia Chase, from 1945 to 1980.

Miss Hermann was an executive with a sharp understanding of audiences. She arrived at ABT at one of the most challenging times in the company's history. A decade of cutbacks in arts funding debilitated the company, which had generated a substantial debt. Moreover, the dancing had begun to seem flaccid. For, while superlative dancers were discovered and nurtured in the Baryshnikov years, their ranks had been buttressed by others who were not especially distinguished. The particular charisma that had typified ABT's performances was seen but rarely.

Miss Hermann acquired several new productions, the most appealing of which was Jiri Kylian's soaring, exuberant *Sinfonietta*. She also commissioned the pulsating *Serious Pleasures*, a compelling work by the gifted Ulysses Dove. Other projects sounded promising but met with limited success: a *Don Quixote* staged by the brilliant Bolshoi danseur Vladimir Vasiliev proved confused and disappointing; a *Coppélia* was ordinary. Attendance at all but a few performances was sketchy. The mood was dark; debt seemed poised to defeat the company. With few exceptions, dancers were downhearted and discouraged.

In the autumn of 1992, a new artistic director was brought to the company. Kevin McKenzie was an unexpected choice, yet an ideal one. Having danced at ABT for most of his career, his life was interwoven with the fabric of the company. Moreover, he was steeped in the company's history and traditions and had abiding respect for them.

At the time of his return to ABT, McKenzie was artistic associate of the Washington Ballet, a company whose high standards he maintained during his two years there. A creature of the studio, he had a voracious appetite for work, an uncanny recall of choreography, the ability to perceive what a dancer was doing wrong, and the knowledge to correct it. As ABT's dancers had come to know, his dedication to ballet was unwavering. And dancers liked and trusted him, which was crucially important in a demoralized company.

An artistic director determines which ballets an audience sees and who they see in them. But he also does much more. The artistic director determines the manner in which dancers will be rehearsed and trained and who will constitute the artistic staff that carries out those vital functions.

Though McKenzie had spent nearly all of his own career as a principal dancer, he had the utmost appreciation for the vital role taken by soloists and the corps de ballet. His overarching intent was to embellish the standards of dancing at every level of the company. Toward that end, he and his artistic staff guided the eighty-five dancers in the company, burnishing, coaxing, correcting, demonstrating steps and mime, elucidating particulars of character and emotion. As the months passed, McKenzie's dancers became a troupe unrivaled by any other company in the world. A few years into his tenure during performances of *La Bayadère* he felt the exhilaration of success. Each night, twenty-four corps de ballet dancers had appeared one by one in the mesmerizing "Shades" scene, holding perfect arabesques and cambré port de bras, then moving on, spectral and lovely in white tutus. As they advanced toward the rim of the stage, the audience broke into sustained applause. It was a moment of enchantment and it had been created by dancers whose names the audience did not know.

A director's personality and mood filter through the company, and this, as much as any other factor, sets the company's tone. McKenzie established a tone that was both crisply professional and encouraging. The dancers had learned from Baryshnikov to expect much from themselves, to focus on details that can turn a passable characterization into a fine one. McKenzie created an ambiance in which they felt secure yet challenged, and so were willing to take the chances necessary for the creation of something astounding.

McKenzie also instituted a collaborative system between the artistic director and the executive director, whom he found first in Gary Dunning, who had held that post with the Houston Ballet, and later in Michael Kaiser, who had recently overseen the spectacular financial turnaround of the Alvin Ailey company. Kaiser had reasoned and articulate ideas about the manner in which a financial turnaround is effected. "The point is to have the funds required to keep your artists producing great art," he noted early on. "Any institution that creates great art can be saved." Together, McKenzie, Kaiser, and the late Peter T. Joseph, chairman of the board of trustees, brought about a resurgence of the company.

Historically, ABT had been a company of stars. With that in mind, McKenzie sought to focus public attention on the principal dancers and build upon the base of those who had advanced upward from the corps de ballet during the Baryshnikov years.

Julie Kent combined an exquisitely fawnlike quality with an unusual facility for illuminating the murkiest corners of the soul and heart; Kathleen Moore was a dramatic ballerina who was never less than stunningly persuasive; Amanda McKerrow blended crystal clear technique with gossamer lightness; Ashley Tuttle danced with a velvety grace that was the essence of femininity; Gil Boggs combined rugged virtuosity with an endearingly impish quality; Christine Dunham's technical polish and uncommon elegance enhanced each role she played; Keith Roberts danced with a force and immediacy that made him a leading interpreter of contemporary works; Robert Hill's dancing was suffused with graciousness.

McKenzie augmented these artists with remarkable dancers from a variety of nations and trainings. Within a few years, the roster included Jose Manuel Carreño, in whom the regal bearing of a *danseur noble* combined with Latin heat; Vladimir Malakhov, a diaphanous creature blessed with the lightness of a feather and a star's requisite aura of mystery; Nina Ananiashvili, whose precision was rivaled only by her fluency; Angel Corella, who arrived at ABT an unknown and became a star in his first performances; and Ethan Stiefel, a dancer with an immaculate classical technique and a captivating manner that melded innocence with knowing.

PHOTO BY ROY ROUND

Julie Kent in *Giselle* (1992)

These artists transformed everyday company classes into displays of gift and grace generally seen only at the sort of gala evening that recruits the stars of numerous companies. Their performances revitalized the perception of the company. A few years into McKenzie's tenure, American Ballet Theatre had become a company with few peers.

McKenzie's directorship differed substantially from Baryshnikov's, in part because they were men of disparate temperaments and tastes, but also because the times in which they led the company were different. When Baryshnikov took over ABT in 1980, the much-heralded "ballet boom" was still in effect. This was an era

Robert Hill as Albrecht in *Giselle* (1994)

of some twenty years that had begun in the early 1960s, heralded by Nureyev's arrival in the West, and amplified by his partnership with Fonteyn, which was a stunning pairing of opposites.

It was an intoxicating time, with great choreographers creating works for great dancers: Ashton created *The Dream* for Antoinette Sibley and Dowell and *Marguerite and Armand* for Nureyev and Fonteyn; Tudor created *The Leaves Are Fading* for Gelsey Kirkland; Robbins created *Other Dances* for Makarova and Baryshnikov; Balanchine and Robbins created a panoply of works for the leading dancers of City Ballet. The ballet audience burgeoned; then time passed, many great careers faded, and the boom ended as precipitously as it began. As a vital element to that boom, Baryshnikov continued to command attention. For better and for worse, he was among the few dancers written about on the dance, gossip, and society pages. All that he did was watched and reported upon. This gave automatic visibility to whatever company he led.

By the time McKenzie assumed the directorship of ABT, the ballet boom was a glowing era consigned to memory. Audience attention had appreciably diminished; where it existed, the preference was for ballet-as-spectacle, that is, for full-length story ballets

PHOTO BY PAUL KOLNIK

Othello with Sandra Brown and Desmond Richardson (1997)

rather than repertory programs composed of several short works on a given evening. To entice audiences back to the theater, McKenzie determined that ballet needed to rival the appeal of the most superlative stage offerings. The full-length works he acquired had the sophisticated production values of Broadway theater, the emotional amplitude of opera, and stunning opportunities for his surfeit of remarkable dancers. Nowhere was this more in evidence than in the 1997 Lar Lubovitch production of *Othello*, a stark and riveting work that, with its original choreography, music, and designs, was the first fully commissioned evening-length ballet in ABT's history. *Othello* was born of an artistic blending that mirrored McKenzie's fascination with all the popular arts, from music to avant-garde stage productions to film. Its dissonant score was created by Eliot Goldenthal, a composer of film scores, among them, *Interview with a Vampire* and *Michael Collins*. The sparse scenery and rich costumes had an opulent, dramatic quality that recalled staged productions of Ingmar Bergman. Lubovitch gave the dancers fiercely disjointed movement; at the premiere performance Othello was brilliantly danced by the company's stunning Desmond Richardson.

McKenzie also embellished a roster of long-favored and familiar ballets, among them *La Bayadère* and *Giselle*, with new full-length pieces, chief among them a revival of Sir Kenneth MacMillan's richly romantic and tragic *Manon*; Ronald Hynd's opulent and witty *The Merry Widow*; Anna-Marie Holmes's sublime rendering of Petipa's *Le Corsaire*; and Ben Stevenson's fantastical *The Snow Maiden*. McKenzie also choreographed several works, including a dazzling and pyrotechnical *Don Quixote* (in a collaboration with Susan Jones) and, for ABT's sixtieth anniversary, his own rendering of *Swan Lake*. All of these sumptuous works provided heightened evenings that turned going to the ballet into an event.

The 1997 spring season at the Metropolitan Opera House was the most financially rewarding season in the company's history. By its conclusion, the burden of debt was eradicated. Artistry and repertory had galvanized contributors and audiences, and transformed ABT's fortunes.

But McKenzie was also determined to retain that distinguished body of works which had given ABT its unique flavor, for he had the greatest respect for the way the company had always styled itself as both a showplace for classics and a commissioner of new works. That fall, he instituted an autumn season at New York's City Center. It was a season designed for this venue, a house which was smaller and more intimate than the Metropolitan Opera House and allowed audiences a closer view of the one-act works with which ABT had long been associated, as well as works that McKenzie had commissioned. For McKenzie, a most significant aspect of this season was that it would acquaint young ABT dancers with their heritage.

For the first season, McKenzie revived *Fancy Free*, a ballet that he had loved dancing, as well as *Fall River Legend* and *The Leaves Are Fading*; these defining ballets for ABT expressed a prodigious range of mood and motion. Several years earlier, McKenzie had revived Tudor's *Echoing of Trumpets*. Now returning another Tudor work to the repertory was a particular pleasure. As a dancer he had been well suited to the dramatic richness and introspection of Tudor's characters, who had culled from him a darker side of his talents. Tudor, McKenzie had long believed, deserved the moniker Baryshnikov had bestowed on him: "the artistic conscience of Ballet Theatre."

At City Center, the company also performed works that Baryshnikov had commissioned: Mark Morris's *Drink to Me Only with Thine Eyes* and Clark Tippet's *Bruch Violin Concerto No. 1*.

Fancy Free with (left to right) Ethan Brown, John Gardner, Angel Corella, Martha Butler, and Sandra Brown (1997)

PHOTO BY ANA VENEGAS

For the second fall season, Twyla Tharp created a new work, *Known by Heart*, which featured a stunningly forceful and masterful pas de deux for Susan Jaffe and Ethan Stiefel. Other new works of note were *Disposition*, commissioned from the ABT dancer John Selya, and *Without Words*, by Nacho Duato, artistic director of Madrid's National Dance Company, whose *Remanso*, created for the first City Center season, attracted praise and attention.

In his first years as director, McKenzie commissioned a number of contemporary ballets for ABT's spring season at the Metropolitan Opera House. Twyla Tharp created *Americans We*, a series of dances set to a suite of nineteenth-century songs that illuminated facets of the American spirit. Her *How Near Heaven*, set to music by Benjamin Britten, was a stunning formal work that advanced her sophisticated use of ballet movement. *The Elements* was rife with Tharp's signature nonstop movement and whimsical humor. James Kudelka's dark and moody *Cruel World* was a meditation on the implausibility of love and attachment; Jiri Kylian's contribution was an intriguingly abstract *Stepping Stones*; Lar Lubovitch set two works on the company that he had made previously—*A Brahms Symphony*, set to Brahms's Symphony No. 3 in F, Op. 90, was a darkly passionate and romantic work that brought to mind some of the earlier Massine symphonic ballets; *The Red Shoes* was a work Lubovitch had choreographed to music by Jule Styne for the recent Broadway production. McKenzie was intent on adding these ballets to the repertory, for he was convinced that only through commissioning new works could a ballet company remain vital.

To dance these varying works, his dancers needed a command of different styles. "You have to be a modern dancer; you have to be a classical dancer," he told company members. "You have to be able to change your style like changing clothes."

While ABT's modern works were danced, for the most part, at City Center, the spring season at the Metropolitan Opera House was dominated by full-length classical ballets. This, in some measure, was a nod to audience preference; it was also a sign that McKenzie regarded the classics as the measure of standard for dancers and for a company. All that season, night after night, these ballets generated a fervor that heralded the possibility of a new ballet boom. During curtain calls, audiences rose to their feet, shouting "Bravo!" and pelting dancers with bouquets of spring flowers. On many occasions the audience remained standing in place even after the house lights went back on. This was another measure of standard. And it was a measure of magic created: an audience so transfixed that it could not quite bear to leave the theater and return to the everyday world.

By the early 1990s, much of the available excitement in ballet was coming from two ABT principal dancers who had forged ballet's most enchanting and significant partnership. This was the pairing of Julio Bocca and Alessandra Ferri, artists who knew how to weave a spell and whose performances were mesmeric. Individually, they were exquisite dancers. Together, they demonstrated that a ballet partnership is a curious alchemy through which two dancers exceed even the sum of their parts.

They melded for reasons that neither could enunciate even if they had cared to. It was, Miss Ferri would say, like falling in love; its causes were too mystical and amorphous to be quantified. In physical terms, the basis of their partnership was more apparent: both were blessed with sublime lyricism and extraordinarily expressive, supple bodies. What they created together was true to life and bigger than life. When they danced, the audience believed whatever they wanted them to believe.

Miss Ferri had been the company's leading dramatic ballerina since joining ABT in 1985. An artist with gorgeously arched feet and deep, expressive eyes, she conveyed the most profound subtleties, complexities, and extremes of character and emotion. As a child, she had been enthralled by music; she was only four when she discovered that dancing enabled her to become part of that music. She trained at Teatro alla Scala before going on to the Royal Ballet School, where Sir Kenneth MacMillan saw in her the ideal ballerina for his most taxing and meaningful works.

Julio Bocca was raised in a poverty-ridden district of Argentina. He, too, was four when he began to dance, studying first with his mother, a dance teacher, then at the Institute of Art at the Colon Theatre in Buenos Aires. A dazzling technician, he was also an artist of uncommon subtlety and feeling. His dancing was distinguished by a fierce interplay between passion and restraint, ferment and control, dualities that Cavaradossi in Puccini's *Tosca* defines as "the sweet harmony of contrast." Nureyev, praising him, described him as a "child of nature."

His Romeo was an impetuous boy who sinks into depths of feeling, while Ferri's Juliet was the blushing yet willful girl that MacMillan intended, for whom falling in love has the tidal power of falling into a trance. Her bashfulness contrasted with his brash insistence, until the balcony pas de deux, in which reticence gives way to abandon.

Bocca and Miss Ferri danced the ABT premiere of another MacMillan ballet, *Manon*, in which she brought a tatty charm to the tempestuous young courtesan Manon, whose bright eyes fix disastrously on the main chance. Bocca's Des Grieux, impassioned and stubborn, was touchingly foolhardy in the way that people can be when they love deeply but unwisely. Their pas de deux were sweet

Alessandra Ferri and Julio Bocca in *Romeo and Juliet* (1988)

PHOTO BY MIRA

Alessandra Ferri and Julio Bocca in *Manon* (1993)

PHOTO BY MARTHA SWOPE

PHOTO BY ANTHONY CRICKMAY

Alessandra Ferri and Julio Bocca in *Giselle* (1990)

PHOTO BY MIRA

Julio Bocca in *La Bayadère* (1991)

and fervent; the downward path of their characters seemed as inevitable as it was horrific.

In the work most associated with their partnership, Ferri's fiercely protective Giselle offered Albrecht forgiveness imbued with beneficence and solemn conviction. Bocca's Albrecht had learned enough by then to recognize that he was undeserving of such grace, even as he basked in it, sought it, craved it. At daybreak, his life spared, he follows Giselle as she retreats to her grave. Dazed, he shakes his head, as if attempting to rid himself of the terrible realization that she will no longer be with him.

Bocca's spectacular gifts expanded as the years passed, as he illuminated full-length ballets for ABT, most notably when he danced Solor in Makarova's *La Bayadère,* a ballet that seemed made for his blend of perfectly executed technique and atavistic passion.

But he could also amuse and beguile an audience as he did in Ronald Hynd's delightful *The Merry Widow.* Partnering Christine Dunham, Bocca's Count had the superciliousness of one who thinks considerably more of himself than he should, while her Hanna was all beauty and flirtatious wiles.

PHOTO BY PAUL KOLNIK

Christine Dunham and Julio Bocca in *The Merry Widow* (1997)

Miss Dunham joined ABT in 1985 and was promoted to principal dancer four years later in the wake of her fine debut as Odette/Odile in *Swan Lake*. Her loveliness lent a special graciousness to her portrayals of the Queen of the Driads in *Don Quixote*, the Fairy Godmother in Ben Stevenson's *Cinderella*, and *The Sleeping Beauty*'s Lilac Fairy. She was especially delightful in *The Merry Widow*, where her elegance, demureness, and charm were evocative of Dame Margot Fonteyn, who had danced Hanna in the production staged by the Australian Ballet.

Hynd's ballet had all the luscious variety and rich appeal of a tray of Viennese pastries. Entering ABT's repertory in 1997, it offered comedic and virtuoso opportunities for many dancers: one cast had an amusingly intrepid Angel Corella wooing a lithesome Ashley Tuttle while Gil Boggs did his own comic turn as the Ambassador's aide, Njegus. On opening night, the leading roles were danced by Susan Jaffe and her frequent partner, Jose Manuel Carreño.

Susan Jaffe had come a long distance from the corps girl selected, nearly two decades earlier, to dance "Pas d'Esclave" with Alexander Godunov. She had risen swiftly at ABT, having joined the company in 1980, becoming a soloist one year later, and a principal in 1983. She applied herself to her craft and art with uncommon focus and determination, seeking from ABT's incisive ballet mistresses a schooling in essentials and nuances. Working with Irina Kolpakova she developed purity, a term that delineates a quality not so much precise as it is unadorned. With Georgina Parkinson, she honed her performances, adding to them subtleties and details that she described as "the perfume." In time, she evinced a quality that ballerinas should possess in abundance but

PHOTO BY PAUL KOLNIK

Angel Corella, Ashley Tuttle, and Gil Boggs in *The Merry Widow* (1997)

PHOTO BY ROY ROUND

Susan Jaffe and Jose Manuel Carreño in *The Merry Widow* (1997)

rarely do: a womanliness, with its sensuality, tenderness, knowledge, and compassion.

Her Odette in *Swan Lake* was a poignantly wounded creature; her Odile was darkly triumphant and unyielding. As *La Bayadère*'s Nikiya, she was sinuous and alluring, even as she betrayed her pain. Her Myrta in *Giselle* was a pitiless creature with fixed, hard eyes; her Aurora was effervescent as she grew from girlhood into a young woman transfixed by the miracle of love.

As the company's reigning ballerina, she could have taken an imperial attitude, but she never did. Instead, she was unaffected and direct, qualities that made her a special dancer in contemporary parts. Roles were created for her in *Serious Pleasures, Bruch Violin Concerto No. 1, Cruel World,* and *Americans We.*

Dancing with Jose Manuel Carreño, a Cuban who joined the company at the end of the 1995 season, further intensified Miss Jaffe's work, making her freer and prompting her to explore her roles ever more deeply. With their lambent eyes, full mouths, and sculpted faces, they were a beautiful pair who brought great energy to the stage.

In *Don Quixote* they were vibrantly alive, reveling in each other's presence; in *Swan Lake,* the emphatic force of their passion was restrained by courtliness. As *The Sleeping Beauty*'s Princess Aurora and Prince Florimund they were dazzling exemplars of life, grace, and classicism.

Both had flourished under the directorship of McKenzie, who insisted that dancers develop their individuality. If there was a watershed in Miss Jaffe's career, it came early in McKenzie's tenure when he told her, "Be your own dancer." It was an admonishment that fixed her determination to be what she finally became: an evolving, intelligent artist who could make an audience laugh and weep and could execute thirty-two perfect *fouettés* or a whiplash-quick succession of *chainé* turns.

Partnering Miss Jaffe helped Carreño to attain a level that he had never reached previously. He had always been an arresting presence and fine technician in the years that he danced with the Cuban National Ballet and the Royal Ballet. The ambiance of McKenzie's Ballet Theatre freed him to be the danseur that he had never quite been. As he and Miss Jaffe sought to enrich each successive performance he honed an arresting blend of earthiness and elegance that gave his dancing its particular quality. He brought a sultriness to ballet, and a raw male presence not always associated with men who dance, a presence so potent that he never needed to assert it.

Nowhere was this more apparent than in his portrayal of Ali, the

Susan Jaffe and Jose Manuel Carreño in *Don Quixote* (1995)

PHOTO BY CAROL ROSEGG

slave in *Le Corsaire,* a ballet that provided the apogee of the 1998 spring season for many. A superlative Petipa work, its fantastical tale fastens on the pirate chief Conrad's abduction of the Greek maiden Medora, with whom he falls in love. From the moment Carreño as Ali leapt onto the stage, it was apparent that he had matured, becoming a danseur in the full bloom of his powers.

A product of the training in another part of the world was Nina Ananiashvili, a ballerina with skills and polish that few could equal, who joined American Ballet Theatre in 1993. Born in Tbilisi, Georgia, she began her performing life as a figure skater. By her early teens she had become a serious student of ballet, graduating from the Moscow Ballet School in 1981. She was immediately taken into the Bolshoi. Over the next five years, she won gold medals at the most prestigious international competitions. In those same years, she danced the Bolshoi's expansive repertory, establishing herself as one of those rare ballerinas possessed of delicacy and strength in equal measures, like fine china.

Miss Ananiashvili inhabited each role she played. Her Manon was as enticing as she was ill-fated. The deadly descents of her Juliet and Giselle from joy to death were exquisitely calibrated. In the title role of Ben Stevenson's *The Snow Maiden,* created for her, she was a magical and willful sprite, whose doomed fixation on a Russian prince betrothed to another causes her to melt away. She brought verisimilitude to even this fanciful figure, as her Snow Maiden expands from a playful, headstrong creature to a young woman overwhelmed by desire.

PHOTO BY NANCY ELLISON

Jose Manuel Carreño in *Le Corsaire* (1998)

PHOTO BY JANN WHALEY

Nina Ananiashvili in *The Snow Maiden* (1998)

But her most extraordinary portrayals were the Odette/Odile roles of *Swan Lake*. Her pained, assailable Odette provided a perfect contrast to the brittle assurance of her Odile. In all of these characterizations, she demonstrated the way in which ballet steps can be used to reveal the terrors, yearnings, and methods of the human heart.

Another memorable Odette/Odile was Julie Kent, whose first appreciation of what an artist can achieve on a ballet stage was garnered watching Victor Barbee in Agnes de Mille's *The Informer*. Standing backstage, she saw that he was so subsumed in his portrayal that he had no seeming relation to the person she had come to know. This level of involvement was what she strived for and attained. It could be seen in her debut performance of *Swan Lake*, as she veered between Odette's feathery delicacy and Odile's iron will. For that performance, she was partnered by a rapt Guillaume Graffin, a romantic dancer and a favorite of Nureyev, who hired him for the Paris Opera Ballet when he was very young. Graffin enhanced a ballerina with the presence, taste, and instincts that gave him his special quality.

His abiding interests in philosophy, literature, and art added breadth and humanity to all that he did onstage. His dancing linked passion to refinement; and, in the process, demonstrated ballet's crucial links between thought and emotion, intellect and artistry. These qualities gained praise for his Apollo and lent romance and dignity to his Des Grieux, his Siegfried, his Romeo.

Graffin's exceptional aptitude for character roles derived from his

PHOTO BY MIRA

Nina Ananiashvili and Julio Bocca in *Swan Lake* (1994)

razor-sharp observations of people. His Dr. Coppelius was finicky and overbearing; his Gamache in *Don Quixote* was a silly, dandified figure whose illusions about himself were oddly moving. He and Julie Kent also danced Basilio and Kitri in Act I of the *Don Quixote* choreographed by Kevin McKenzie and Susan Jones, enlivening the roles with style and flamboyance.

The McKenzie-Jones *Don Quixote*, with its ebullient Minkus score, virtuoso variations, delightful character turns, and bright ensemble dancing, was a particular favorite with audiences. For the premiere, Miss Kent appeared as the lovely Queen of the Driads in the enchanting "Vision" scene, dancing with a Don Quixote played by Victor Barbee, whom she had recently married. As she beckoned his Don on to glorious romantic vistas, he followed, eyes aglow, dazed and besotted. Together, they created one of ballet's exquisite, otherworldly moments.

Julie Kent was new to the corps de ballet when her uncommon potential became apparent. With her innate beauty, supreme graciousness, command of classical style, and ability to bewitch an audience, she was all that a ballerina should be. She was also a dedicated worker who perpetually sought to improve, increase her stamina, deepen her characterizations, and force herself beyond all that came readily. The result was captivating: her Aurora had the glint of diamonds; her beguiling Medora in *Le Corsaire* was augmented with sly humor; her exquisite Juliet was delicate, sweet, and heartrending as she trod the path from innocence to awareness to misery.

PHOTO BY MIRA

Julie Kent and Guillaume Graffin in *Swan Lake* (1993)

Miss Kent had the artistry and imagination to be fully alive onstage, to be willing to go wherever characterization, music and steps could take her. This was especially apparent in Act III of *Romeo and Juliet*, when her abandoned, betrayed Juliet sits at the foot of her bed, a small and terrified figure, who remains perfectly still as the music swells and her thoughts race. It was moments like this one that elevated her work and made it unforgettable.

On many occasions, Miss Kent danced with Vladimir Malakhov, who joined ABT as a principal dancer in the spring of 1995. Born in the Ukraine, Malakhov began his training there at the age of four; six years later, he went on to the Bolshoi School in Moscow. Upon graduation in 1986, he joined the Moscow Classical Ballet as the company's youngest principal dancer. By the time he arrived at ABT, he had established an international reputation in the first rank of danseurs through his association with the Vienna Ballet.

His exotic, arresting presence resulted from his facility for being catlike and princelike simultaneously. In him, many saw echoes of Nijinsky's otherworldly grace, androgynous affect, and intensity. His technique was pure, with a jump of stunning height that he followed by suspending himself in the air before landing in silence.

Malakhov was of the old school, a dancer who performed with elegance and with flash and gave his characters more than a trace of melodrama. It was a style in keeping with his essential aesthetic, which was to dance in the way that Callas sings. He sought to incorporate into his own work the clarity and individuality that had distinguished Callas; to see him dance was to recognize that he had succeeded in these aims.

He always regretted that Makarova had retired from ballet before he could partner her. Perhaps that is what gave his Solor in her *La Bayadère* its heightened quality, especially in the "Shades" scene, when he danced with the winged urgency of one trying to fuse with a ghostly presence.

For each role, he took great care in his preparations, readying himself to dance Apollo, for instance, by studying photographs of

PHOTO BY MIRA

Julie Kent and Vladimir Malakhov in *Romeo and Juliet* (1996)

Nureyev in the part. His favorite role was Albrecht, whom he maintained was not a cad but a youth in love with Giselle, unaware of the disastrous consequences that his love could have.

Malakhov often partnered Amanda McKerrow, who joined the company in 1982. At age eighteen, she had been the first American dancer to win the gold medal at the prestigious Moscow International Ballet Competition. Miss McKerrow enhanced her immaculate technique with a blithe spirit and fluidity that made her equally affecting in Balanchine's *Theme and Variations* and in Tudor's *The Leaves Are Fading.* She always regarded working with Tudor as "a gift" that provided one of the brightest spots of her professional life.

From the start, Miss McKerrow was a consummate professional who went about her work with conviction, endurance, and fearlessness. She danced all the classical roles, infusing life into characters as diverse as *Coppélia*'s vivacious Swanilda and the conniving Gamzatti of *La Bayadère.* Later in her career, when she was partnered by Malakhov and by Julio Bocca, her dancing took on a certain passion and fire. She also danced beautifully with her husband, the ABT soloist John Gardner; together, they appeared to be a seamless blend of body and mind.

Gil Boggs was a virtuoso dancer endowed with boyish, natural charm. Having entered ABT's corps de ballet in 1982, he became a principal dancer nine years later. An unusually accomplished actor, he brought radiance and reality to every role he danced. When the curtain rose on the first act of *Manon* to reveal his Lescaut sitting alone on the stage, he swiftly established a mood of anticipation and menace that set the tone for the evening. In act two, his

Vladimir Malakhov in *Swan Lake* (1996)

PHOTO BY MIRA

PHOTO BY ANTHONY CRICKMAY

Amanda McKerrow in *The Leaves Are Fading* (1990)

PHOTO BY ROY ROUND

Vladimir Malakhov in *La Bayadère* (1996)

PHOTO BY MARTHA SWOPE

Kathleen Moore and Gil Boggs in *Manon* (1993)

drunken dance was comedic perfection that began in his glazed eyes and extended to his unsteady feet. His Mercutio was a devilish, irrepressible figure whose death was strangely horrifying and moving. Boggs left ABT for a year to dance in Twyla Tharp's company; his performances in her works, and in other contemporary ballets, from *A Brahms Symphony* to his Champion Roper in *Rodeo*, were always exceptionally intense and vivid. His dancing seemed effortless, and he never ceased to be one of those dancers whom audiences love watching.

As Lescaut, Boggs often danced with Kathleen Moore, who brought her appealing spiritedness and uncommon acting ability to the role of Lescaut's mistress. Like Boggs, Miss Moore joined ABT in 1982 and became a principal dancer in 1991. Her range was extraordinary. From her agonized performance in Tudor's *Echoing of Trumpets* to her finely drawn portrait of The Accused in *Fall River Legend*, to her brief turn as Apollo's mother, she imbued all that she did with integrity and meaning. She enhanced many performances of *Giselle* with her darkly arresting Myrta and her watchful, warning mother. As The Girl in *The Informer*, a role that de Mille created for her, she was preternaturally intent and focused. Roles were also created for her in *Drink to Me Only with Thine Eyes*, *The Elements*, and *How Near Heaven*. She was the sort of

PHOTO BY MARTHA SWOPE

Kathleen Moore and Victor Barbee in *The Informer* (1988)

performer who comes along rarely, whose immaculate technique was matched by an ability to portray a character's complexity and nuance.

Another dancer who joined ABT in 1982 was Robert Hill, a refined and elegant danseur who approached his roles with marked intelligence. An accomplished classical dancer and attentive partner, he took a leave from ABT to dance with several distinguished companies, among them New York City Ballet, the Royal Ballet, and the Ballet Teatro alla Scala, returning to Ballet Theatre in 1993 as a principal dancer. He was noteworthy in contemporary works, several of which were created on him, giving his expressiveness a fresh forum. The pas de deux in *Cruel World*, which James Kudelka choreographed on Hill and Julie Kent, made maximal use of her diaphaneity and his strength and solidity.

In Lar Lubovitch's *Othello*, Hill imbued Iago with the overweening evil and twisted authority that had made that character an abiding synonym for wickedness. As the prince in *The Sleeping Beauty* and *Swan Lake* he danced with courtliness and fluidity.

Toward the end of the century, American Ballet Theatre raised several more dancers to principal dancer status. Ashley Tuttle and Keith Roberts both joined the corps de ballet in 1987. McKenzie made each a principal ten years later. Miss Tuttle danced with

PHOTO BY PAUL KOLNIK

Susan Jaffe and Robert Hill in *Othello* (1997)

delicacy, profound musicality and a harmonious mastery of classical style that enhanced the many roles in which she appeared, among them *The Sleeping Beauty*'s Aurora, the title role in *Cinderella*, the "Peasant Pas de Deux" in *Giselle*, as well as the title role, which she danced with sweetness and beauty that touched the heart. As Amour in *Don Quixote*, she was an adorable, cherubic sprite; to the leading ballerina role in *Theme and Variations* she brought the requisite blend of sharp precision and womanly grace; to John Selya's *Disposition* she brought a daring readiness to seem out of control onstage.

Keith Roberts had a dervishlike speed and a dramatic flair, from the wide-eyed freshness of his rendering of The Boy in *The Red Shoes* to the solemn regality that distinguished his *Othello* to the exuberance of his sailor in *Fancy Free*, to his provocative turn in *Stepping Stones*. His particular talents and partnering skills made him especially well suited for contemporary works. As a result, roles were created for him in *Americans We, Cruel World, How Near Heaven*, and *The Elements*.

In the 1990s three new ABT principals, Paloma Herrera, Angel Corella, and Ethan Stiefel, generated the excitement reserved for the most promising of dancers.

Paloma Herrera, who had dreamed, as a ballet student in Argentina, of joining ABT, was taken into the company in 1991 as a

PHOTO BY ROSALIE O'CONNOR

Ashley Tuttle in *The Sleeping Beauty* (1997)

member of the corps de ballet. She was just fifteen. The previous year, Miss Herrera had reached the final round at the Fourteenth International Ballet Competition in Varna, Bulgaria. One of the judges was Natalia Makarova, who invited her to take class with the English National Ballet. She soon moved on to the School of American Ballet; after just six months of study, she danced the leading role in *Raymonda* at the school's annual workshop performance, in the wake of which she was offered a position at ABT.

She was eighteen when she made her debut in Balanchine's *Theme and Variations*, exhibiting unusual technical finesse. Stunningly fleet footwork and astounding balances soon became her signature. These attributes were given full range in *Don Quixote* and *The Sleeping Beauty* with her glittering renderings of Kitri and Aurora. Miss Herrera's prodigious technique was also put to use in contemporary works as she created leading roles in *Cruel World* and Twyla Tharp's *How Near Heaven* and *Americans We*.

She often danced with Angel Corella, who noted her voracious appetite for movement: holding her body in his hands, he said, he could feel her readiness to go for broke. Together, they were extraordinary in the pas de deux created on them in Tharp's *Americans We*, in Balanchine's *Tchaikovsky Pas de Deux*, and in

PHOTO BY PAUL KOLNIK

Andrei Dokukin and Keith Roberts in *Stepping Stones* (1996)

PHOTO BY PAUL KOLNIK

The Elements (1996) with Martha Butler and Keith Roberts

Don Quixote, works in which audiences were captivated by their glistening youth, unrestrained energy, and ebullience.

When Angel Corella came to ABT in 1995 he was nineteen years old, an unknown dancer who had spent several years in the National Ballet of Spain, a company run by the superlative teacher Victor Ullate. Having recently won the grand prize and the gold medal at an international dance competition in Paris, he too came to the attention of Miss Makarova, who made a fervent recommendation on his behalf to Kevin McKenzie. This resulted in McKenzie taking the unusual step of bringing Corella into the company as a soloist just prior to the spring season, giving him roles in ballets that had long been cast and weathering the predictable protests of other dancers. McKenzie never questioned the wisdom of those actions. "When you see that energy for the first time . . ." he recalled halfway through the 1995 season, still buoyed by the pleasure of it. "Around here, the going joke was, 'But can he sing?'"

From his first performance, in *Giselle*'s "Peasant Pas de Deux," Corella created a sensation. His elegant *épaulement,* archingly graceful *port de bras,* effortless *ballon,* and soft landings were enhanced by the obvious, unfettered joy he took in dancing. "When I dance, I feel as if I am being moved by something outside myself," he said."It is the feeling of being a puppet." Performing, he said, "is like being in love for the first time, and being loved back."

His debut in *Theme and Variations,* at the close of his first season, was an event at which Corella could either dash the immense expectations placed on him or justify them. As the curtain rose, the

PHOTO BY MIRA

Paloma Herrera in *Theme and Variations* (1994)

PHOTO BY ROY ROUND

Paloma Herrera and Angel Corella in *Americans We* (1995)

PHOTO BY MIRA

Paloma Herrera and Angel Corella in *Don Quixote* (1996)

PHOTO BY ROSALIE O'CONNOR

Angel Corella in *Romeo and Juliet* (1998)

PHOTO BY ANA VENEGAS

Angel Corella in *Coppélia* (1997)

PHOTO BY NANCY ELLISON

Susan Jaffe and Ethan Stiefel in *Le Corsaire* (1998)

PHOTO BY PAUL KOLNIK

Ethan Stiefel in *Known by Heart* (1998)

excitement in the audience was palpable; by the time the curtain descended, the audience's expectations had been exceeded. As time went on, Corella's fierce hunger for roles of every shading and style established him as a danseur who, like Baryshnikov before him, had no limits.

His repertory quickly came to include the major roles, from Solor in *La Bayadère* to Romeo, Albrecht in *Giselle*, Franz in *Coppélia*, Basilio in *Don Quixote*, and Conrad and Ali in *Le Corsaire*. In each role, Corella evinced his technique's stunning proportions. In one performance after another, it was apparent that his razor-sharp turns and airborne velocity would set new standards for danseurs in the coming century.

The other young dancer setting new standards was Ethan Stiefel, a very different dancer than Corella, though no less gifted. Like Corella, Stiefel had been dazzled by the dancing of Mikhail Baryshnikov. By the time he joined ABT at the age of twenty-four he was regarded as the most exciting American-born dancer to come along since Edward Villella's arrival in the early 1960s.

A protégé of Stanley Williams at the School of American Ballet, Steifel joined New York City Ballet at the age of sixteen, where he swiftly took on major roles and was coached by Baryshnikov for his debut in *Harlequinade*. He mastered many roles in the Balanchine and Robbins repertory, chief among them his elegant Apollo, his dynamic rendering of the pas de deux in *Stars and Stripes*, and his winsome turn in *Dances at a Gathering*.

He left City Ballet and came to ABT in 1997, joining the company as a principal dancer and bringing to his work an intense musicality, sharp attack, and a flawless, understated technique, with its perfect turns and magnificent jump. Onstage, Stiefel was an astonishing presence with a sweetness tempered by a hint of danger. Within his first two years in the company, he was enhancing all the leading male parts. After his debut as Albrecht in *Giselle*, Clive Barnes predicted that Stiefel would be the first great Albrecht of the twenty-first century. He brought to ballet an irresistible combination: he danced with deep intelligence, considering each role so thoroughly that he apprehended the thoughts that underlay even the slightest movement; at the same time, he danced with the entirety of his ample spirit and his heart.

American Ballet Theatre, under the directorship of Kevin McKenzie, is the result of a lengthy evolution that goes on and on, for, as those who make their life in the ballet know, the work of a company never ceases. To visit the rehearsal studios of Ballet Theatre on any given day is to see an art taught by its gifted former practitioners to the gifted who are still youthful enough to dance it. In one studio, Georgina Parkinson coaches Julie Kent in the MacMillan roles Miss Parkinson once danced; in another studio, Irina Kolpakova coaches Susan Jaffe and Ethan Stiefel in *Giselle*, a ballet in which Miss Kolpakova established herself as a leading ballerina of the Kirov. In nearby studios, Victor Barbee teaches the High Brahmin's mime to corps de ballet boys who hope that the part will be their opportunity, while David Richardson rehearses *Tchaikovsky Pas de Deux* with Paloma Herrera and Angel Corella. In another studio, Kevin McKenzie reviews his *Don Quixote* choreography with Nina Ananaishvili and Julio Bocca.

THE SPIRITS of the dancers who have gone abide in the dancers who remain. The repertory offers pleasures and education for audiences and for the company. All this is good for ABT and it is good for ballet itself. In that sense, these artists and the works they dance are American Ballet Theatre's contribution to the art to which its members, present and past, have devoted themselves. It is an art that has everything to show, and much to give.

Jiri Kylian's *Sinfonietta* (1991)

PHOTO BY PAUL KOLNIK